CRACKING THE IT CODE

Technology Management for Non-Technology Managers

Anthony L. Butler

INDIE BOOKS
INTERNATIONAL

No part of this publication may be reproduced or distributed in any forms or any means, without the prior permission of the publisher. Requests for permission should be directed to permissions@indiebooksintl.com, or mailed to Permissions, Indie Books International, 2424 Vista Way, Suite 316, Oceanside, CA 92054.

Neither the publisher nor the author is engaged in rendering legal or other professional services through this book. If expert assistance is required, the services of appropriate professionals should be sought. The publisher and the author shall have neither liability nor responsibility to any person or entity with respect to any loss or damage caused directly or indirectly by the information in this publication.

ISBN: 1-941870-12-0
ISBN 13: 978-1-941870-12-9
Library of Congress Control Number: 2015931106

Designed by Joni McPherson, mcphersongraphics.com

INDIE BOOKS INTERNATIONAL, LLC
2424 VISTA WAY, SUITE 316
OCEANSIDE, CA 92054
www.indiebooksintl.com

For all of the entrepreneurs trying to make their mark.

My deepest hope is that *Cracking the IT Code* will help you focus on your core business.

Table of Contents

●————————————●

Acknowledgements

My deepest thank you to everyone who contributed to my thinking, the process and completion of the book; most notably, my entire Vistage Group and Mark Taylor, our chair and leader. Also, thank you to Hollis Buffered, Dan Hoffman, Brian Klansky, Cahal Grennan, Dan Pink, Geoffrey Moore, Seth Godin, and Dan Kennedy.

And most especially, a big thank you to my loving wife, Tatiana Butler for her awesome infographics and tough love pushing me to finish the project. Without her help it would still be gathering dust on my shelf.

CHAPTER ONE

•————————————•

The Riddle

"Introducing new technology alone is never enough. The big spurts in productivity come when new technology is combined with new ways of doing business."
—THOMAS FRIEDMAN, *THE WORLD IS FLAT*

For most managers technology is a mystery. It seems to endlessly eat away at profit, hampers productivity, and can bring business to its knees with outages. It almost feels like a crime in progress conducted by three super villains: Money Pit, The Productivity Bandit, and that business destroyer: Outage. Businesses are in a constant struggle with the evil triad that continues to rear up over and over again.

The riddle for every business is how to spend the right amount on information technology (IT) while ensuring outstanding productivity and minimizing downtime. It entails understanding the implications of the investment toward risk management purposes but also for productivity and efficiency.

The technology landscape is a confusing morass of technical and marketing jargon. Never before has it been so easy for a company to make a poor technology decision that cascades through the entire business. Good, actionable information is hard to find.

Executives are turning to the technology community for expert advice. Often the advice is correct in and of itself, but in the context of the business plan it is often flat out wrong; or possibly worse, it is self-serving to the person giving the advice and comes with costly and often dangerous bias.

Technology for technology's sake is meaningless. It must have more utility than just a certain "cool" factor. In the last few years, dozens of new technologies have inundated the market with an incredible amount of hype and little clarity to their actual usefulness to a business. A large number of marketing tag lines have been introduced with very little real explanation of their meaning. SaaS, VaaS, virtualization, VoIP, social media, cloud computing—the list is quite long and getting longer every day.

Hidden behind the jargon and hype are real benefits for businesses and part of the difficulty is in separating the hype from pragmatic useful tools. Various technologies are opening new doors of opportunity for middle marketing and small businesses that only a few years ago were available only to the largest enterprises with the biggest budgets. For example, real time marketing, customer, and sales data are available to companies smart enough to integrate and implement the right technologies.

Technology is the cornerstone of nearly all business innovation in this decade. It is helping large companies leverage data to deliver intimate customer service in ways that were nearly impossible before. And small and medium businesses can afford advanced technology if they can only understand how.

Technology is improving at an exponential rate and the rate of change itself is accelerating as well. This accelerated rate of change is an important leadership challenge. It requires leaders to rethink how they do business. It needs to be part of the strategic plan in selecting the technology tools of the business and how they are purchased, leased, or subscribed to.

Much of the resistance to adopting new technologies and adopting new ways of doing business are more philosophical and even emotional in nature than pragmatic. Many executive teams have difficulty releasing control of a major business function that can be handled by their own people or infrastructure. Outsourcing a portion of their IT or subscribing to a SaaS program goes against much of their view of the business world. Owning and controlling a function on the surface seems safer and more cost effective. Business as usual feels right. They cloak the insecurity of changing their way of doing business inside concerns about security, performance, disaster recovery, and costs.

There is also some subtle sabotage by in-house technology professionals aiding the three villains. They are currently the trusted advisors business leaders rely on for their technology advice. But technology professionals are often threatened by the very technologies they support. Cloud services are quickly rendering the need for in-house IT professionals obsolete. Their job functions can be mostly automated and as software improves the issues they used to address are in sharp decline. Why does a company need them if technology is finally becoming seamlessly easy to use?

The cost structure of cloud services and emerging virtual technologies makes employing in-house IT professionals much more expensive than before: in many cases, these services make them unnecessary altogether. Technology professionals by and large are terrified of the future. The cloud is most likely the death knell of their entire profession. Very few IT professionals have the courage to recommend that their job be eliminated or outsourced to a cloud service and you have to be on guard with their recommendations.

After engaging with thousands of executives and realizing how poorly most of them understood what they were buying for their business, I realized there is a need for a practical how-to guide to the basics of technology management. Often executives relied on biased information from their technology advisor and didn't know the right questions to ask to get the desired result. The purpose of this book is to help you unravel the IT riddle and make sound decisions toward controlling costs, maximizing productivity, and minimizing downtime.

This book gives a basic understanding and foundation of IT management from the standpoint of what work needs to be done and how to calculate the risks, as well as a basic understanding of the issues facing a company from a technological standpoint.

Understanding why certain issues will crop up in a stage of growth will help to plan for them and remove technology friction from the business, as well as save countless hours of lost time or over investment. The goal is to explain the basics of technology management and to act as a prism through which to weigh the risks versus benefits of a particular technology without delving into the deep technical details. The next chapter will help you understand the basic IT Conundrum and how to start to unravel it.

CLUES TO CRACKING THE CODE

▶ Seek to understand the why behind any technology decision.

▶ Beware of advice with an agenda.

▶ Disregard technology marketing hype; find the business case.

CHAPTER TWO

●━━━━━━━━●

The Conundrum

I n 1989, I enlisted in the US Army and served as an enlisted soldier for three years before applying and being accepted at The United States Military Academy at West Point. After graduation in 1996, I followed the normal career path of an Infantryman: Infantry Officers Basic and Advanced courses, Ranger School, Airborne School, and the Air Assault School. I also served in a number of leadership positions of ever increasing responsibility that were right in my sweet spot of expertise. I was becoming an expert in conducting combat operations.

And then the army threw me a wild pitch. Shortly after being promoted to Captain and while waiting for a company command to open up, I was assigned as the Battalion Motor Officer of a headquarters company of a Mechanized Infantry Battalion. I was put in charge of more than a hundred mechanics, several different types of engineers, fuel experts, and a fleet of heavy machines from tanks, Bradley Fighting Vehicles, M113 tracked vehicles, to HMMWVs, tow trucks, and mortar vehicles. The job was way, way out of my expertise.

And to top it off, I was the officer responsible for managing the senior non-commissioned officers who ran the motor pool and a Chief Warrant Officer 3, all of whom were older than me and had worked in their fields for their entire careers. I was the least qualified person you can imagine for the job, and I was terrified of failing. My background didn't include any expertise in what they were doing on a day to day basis and I was 100 percent responsible for their results. The Army is somewhat uncompromising when it comes to results and it was very much a sink or swim situation. I had to figure out what to do—and quickly.

Luckily for me, the Warrant Officer was not only a deep technical expert, he was also a real leader. He took me under his wing, even though I theoretically outranked him, and he taught me a leadership lesson that has stuck with me for life. His idea was that I only had to be the expert at one thing—asking smart questions. I needed to learn the basics of the daily work but not the details. He taught me that curiosity about what was going on around me would lead me down the right path. The idea was that in the technical world, most people know what needs to happen and asking the right questions will help them clarify their thinking and elevate the status of key resource allocations. Questions help leaders evaluate the work being done from a managerial context and improve decision making.

So, instead of managing the results of the work, I focused on asking questions about the daily activities that lead to the results we needed. After some trial and error, I was able to come up with a series of questions that helped me understand the proper resources needed to get any job done and to find obstacles in the path of the teams. My role became chief facilitator. I made sure everyone had what they needed to be successful on a daily basis, such as tools, man power, and technical resources. I was able to help the teams refine and improve internal processes by asking tough questions about the processes—not the work—and then I helped them answer the questions to improve the overall result. It was an eye opening process and it produced stunning improvements in work flow.

The conundrum in most companies comes in two parts. First, just like when I took over in the motor pool, managers don't understand what needs to be done behind the scenes. They don't know the right questions to ask of the technical team to ensure the right work is being done. Second, the technical team, because of the way it is structured and evaluated, has an inherent conflict of interest in changing the environment for the better. The two issues combined are a recipe for poor decision making.

In most companies the same process I used in the motor pool will lead management teams to success. They need to first understand the basic IT tasks and challenges and then learn the right questions to ask in order to have the right information on which to base resource decisions. The chapters that follow outline the basics of IT management and, after each major subject, include a few key questions to get you started. Every company is slightly different and will have some unique IT needs and these questions can act as a baseline for management teams to develop their own questions that lead to success in their own key performance indicators.

The Conundrum

Take a moment to imagine a small company that is focused on growing its core business. The management team is pushing hard for increased productivity, increased sales, and clients who are happier than ever. When they were a start-up, the CEO and his partner bought a couple of computers themselves, loaded software on them, and hooked them up to the Internet. They did everything themselves. As the company grew, they saved money in do-it-yourself mode until one day the CEO just couldn't handle all of the day-to-day headaches of IT anymore and hired Hal, who was a friend of his cousin. Now Hal was a hardworking guy and smart as they come. He grew up working on computers for himself, friends, and family and took a few courses online to learn how to do more. He even went out and got a couple of low level certifications in computer networking and a certification of the newest operating system, which at the time was Windows Vista.

The first few months Hal was at the company were fantastic. He was a miracle worker. He fixed all of the company's computer related problems. He was fast and responsive. He took calls at all hours of the night and on weekends. He was great and everything ran smoother than ever before.

Over the next couple of years, the company continued to grow. The CEO realized he could magnify the company's growth even faster and he built a marketing department. The new marketing team was extremely talented and creative, but they were unhappy with Windows. It just didn't support the programs they needed to run in their job functions and they were all Mac people and so the company bought two different types of Apple computers.

Also by this time, new employees were receiving new desktops and some executives who worked from home were receiving laptop computers, but they were on the newest operating system, Windows XP. The new laptops had to support specialized software to log onto the server remotely from home, but when everyone logged on from home, the company didn't have enough bandwidth on its Internet connection and so needed to upgrade, which cost a lot.

Then the company opened up a satellite location in a town more than an hour from the main office, and Hal took up support of that office too. Hardworking Hal was working harder than ever, and he was proud of the job he was doing, but there was trouble in paradise. Hal was exhausted and after he took more than a dozen calls while on vacation at Disneyland with the family, he knew he had to ask for help. He just couldn't keep up with the demands of the company. There were just too many problems, too much chaos, and it was more than one man could handle.

Hal went to the CEO and asked for help. The CEO frowned and replied, "Hal, I have started to hear grumbling in the ranks about IT problems. I understand you are working hard, but we just can't afford to hire another IT person full time. I need you to buckle down and work a bit harder. The best I can do for you is give you a part time resource, for 15-20 hours a week, but I will need you to squeeze the cost out of your budget somewhere else. It is just not in the cards to spend more on IT."

Hal was happy to get some help but something bothered him. He was working harder than ever, and he just never seemed to be able to catch up. He knew he needed to take some additional courses but he couldn't find the time while carrying his heavy work load. He needed a change. Hal helped the new part timer on board while he found a new job and left the company a couple of months later.

The short story above is fictional but based in reality in companies across the country. Hardworking Hal is a real phenomenon. The complexity of IT environments can, over time, outpace the expertise and ability of a single person to manage them effectively and the result for the business is poor network performance, security liability, and loss of productivity. The personal cost for technology professionals is burnout and career risk. Nobody wins.

Managing technology for a business takes specific knowledge of the core business and the technology components themselves: hardware, software, and the Internet. Once you understand the main tasks that need to be accomplished, it can be managed seamlessly and at a price point that makes sense for the business.

More often than not, IT is viewed only as a cost center that needs to be managed and not as a process. Management of the technology team is often delegated to an executive who may or may not have an IT back ground. These executives often do not manage the *process* of IT and only manage the results. They are always smart, well-meaning people, but it is not their expertise and they are usually focused on their core function that already has them very busy. The manager often struggles to find the time to properly manage IT or to ask the right questions about issues that arise and it is very easy for them to make a mistake or unintentionally overspend.

Hiring and maintaining an IT team is unlike any other business function. It rarely has anything to do with the core business, and often no one on the management team has a solid grasp of how to manage all of the technologies the business uses. They don't understand the right questions to ask when making purchasing decisions and the information available to them is primarily marketing spin or advice with an agenda. When research is limited to Google searches, the results are often limited to heavy traffic marketing messages, which makes it very difficult for managers with limited knowledge to understand how to make a good decision.

When technology is a necessary evil and not strategic to the core business, it doesn't get a deep focus from the management team because there is just not time to focus on it. Technology is not planned from the start. It is implemented at the lowest cost possible just to get things working in a haphazard way and it isn't until there is enough internal pain of different technologies not working correctly that the management team will decide to hire their first IT guy or look to hire an outside consultant to help them.

The way IT professionals are often evaluated contributes to risk aversion within the department. More often than not, no one from outside the department really understands the difficulty and amount of work to be done in the department nor the skill sets needed to accomplish the tasks at hand correctly. The lack of understanding causes a sort of odd dynamic in the company. As long as IT is up and running, no one outside of the IT team gives it a second thought. There are no ongoing checks and balances that ensure system level management is even occurring. It is possible, and not altogether unusual, for a system to go unmanaged for months.

For example, I was invited to consult for a large retailer headquartered in New York City. A venture capital firm that had invested in the chain—with visions of taking the fifty-seven current locations and scaling the chain world wide—wanted a check up on the IT systems they were using and advice on developing a strategy. They had a laundry list of IT problems that ran the gamut of slow Internet connections at some locations to phone system failures and many complaints surrounding the e-mail system. During the discovery phase of our engagement, I interviewed their two in-house IT personnel.

These two gentlemen were responsible for managing the following:

- Infrastructure management of fifty-seven retail stores, and a headquarters of approximately forty-five employees. This included security, backups, e-mail, patching, firewall management, virus protection, etc.

- Phone systems at fifty-seven locations—more than thirty locations were on different systems.

- Managing the POS systems at each location. This included not only the infrastructure but the business analyst portion. For instance, if a coupon promotion was going on they would add the coupon codes to the system and troubleshoot nationwide.

- They were on call every day and hour because that is when the retail locations were open.

- New store openings nationwide. They were planning four new openings that year and each opening required three to four days of travel, as well as planning time and an enormous amount of correspondence with architects and general contractors to ensure all aspects of IT at each location were set up correctly.

- Desktop support for more than 700 employees nationwide —again, around the clock.

Does this sound a little overwhelming? This only includes the big tasks—there was much more.

On the first day, we discovered the backup system not only wasn't hooked up, but it hadn't worked in months, and all of the servers were out of warranty. The newest server was more than five years old. The phone system was more than fifteen years old and could not support the number of users needed. The company routinely had e-mail problems. There was no standard model of computer in the company and departments were allowed to purchase their own equipment without real input from the IT department. All in all, it was an IT train wreck. Both of their guys were really hardworking and smart, but they were in overwhelm mode. They only worked on fires. They were terribly understaffed and the fires were all they could possibly accomplish in a sixty hour work week. I interviewed them both separately and one of them told me he hadn't had a real vacation in three years and was on the verge of a personal meltdown.

And the kicker was the retailer had just hired a new president to run operations and she wanted to fire both IT guys for incompetence. When I interviewed her, she told me she hadn't seen such "terrible IT service," in her entire career. She wasn't wrong. The company's IT management was a train wreck. But it also wasn't the fault of the IT department. The management team did not fundamentally understand the tasks to be done. They didn't understand the IT resources needed to maintain the system they had or how to manage it, and since it went unmanaged it was neglected until there was an emergency.

The president had no idea of the real scope of what the company asked two people to be responsible for because she had no idea of the work to be done. She evaluated them based on the speed of their responses to her personal issues. She was absolutely correct that their response to her requests were inadequate for her needs. It took them four days after request to import her contacts to Outlook and to get her e-mail set up on her iPhone. She e-mailed the IT team at all hours of the day for support because that is when she and several other executives needed support. What she didn't think through was their ability to respond in a timely manner in the context of all of their other responsibilities. It didn't matter that the team was in Las Vegas opening a new location. Her measurement of performance was responsiveness to end users because that is all that she knew how to measure. What she didn't understand was the enormity of what the company asked them to accomplish and user support was a tiny sliver of the overall picture.

I use this example of IT mismanagement at the extreme end of what can go wrong over a long period of time. But a similar scenario plays itself out in companies every day. Companies in general are very poor at scoping IT duties and responsibilities and managing workloads in a reasonable manner and it shows in the high amount of turnover of IT professionals and the relative difficulty of managing IT in a company over time.

In the example above, the president didn't have a solid grasp of how her IT team should be evaluated. They were being judged by the end results of years of mismanagement that they had no real ability to affect. The very structure of their department and the lack of understanding of the leadership team created the situation. She would have been much better off managing the day-to-day process than just judging the end result. Results matter, but process matters much more as a good process over the long term will produce a desirable result.

Lacking other meaningful performance metrics, IT teams are typically judged by how they react to emergencies because emergencies are what the management team can physically see. The emergencies are the symptoms of the underlying decay of the system and as long as there are enough bandages available, everyone is happy. Handling executive's iPhone issues at 10:00 p.m. wins kudos from the management team, but it is actually the wrong measurement of performance of the team unless that is their main objective and responsibility. But what about the daily task requirements of security, patching, and backups?

Another issue compounding the conundrum is budget. Since the 2008 downturn, IT budgets have been squeezed year after year. Overworked teams are continually being asked to do more with less. Companies are continually asking their IT teams to lower costs. Instead of asking the question, "How much should we be investing?" they are asking, "How do we lower costs?" But if they are already in cost-cutting mode and try to cut costs even more than the resultant shortcuts and shoddy work have long-term consequences.

A result of under investment in IT is teams that are struggling to support legacy hardware that have compatibility issues. Hardware that is long past warranty is being utilized with a hope and a prayer. IT managers deploy short-term "fixes" just to keep the wheels turning, although in many cases the fixes cause more long-term problems and end up increasing support costs rather than if the correct investment was made in the beginning.

Difficulty Staying Relevant

As in the example of Hal's working life, working without the proper resources can make the day-to-day work life of in-house IT professionals a difficult one. They have many competing requirements that force them to become generalists. Because they are asked to handle many different technologies it is very difficult to be a deep expert in any one discipline and still be proficient in several others. The lack of deep technical expertise introduces risk into the environment and increases the time to resolution. A lot of time is spent in researching the root cause of issues. The results are inefficiency, mistakes, and risk.

The day-to-day time crunch is further exasperated by project work. Each project, for the most part, is being done for the first time by the team. It takes research, testing, and preparation to handle a project properly and that is in addition to everything else already going on. The daily activities of the business tend to eat up all of the available work week and finding the time to take additional training courses and certifications to prepare for an upcoming project becomes fantastically difficult—if not impossible. It is not unusual for in-house IT teams to routinely work fifty to sixty hour weeks as the norm, and that is just what they clock. It doesn't include research done in their spare time just to stay current on changes in technology. Much of their work is done late at night and on weekends and finding the time to study and still have a life is often too much for even the most dedicated professionals.

The price of always being judged by their response to emergencies and a tight job market has had an adverse effect on the behavior of IT teams. Many feel under the gun and want to protect their jobs at all costs. The pressure has made them extremely risk adverse and addicted to firefighting. They want to stay under the radar and avoid being noticed unless it is to reduce the budget in some way.

In many cases, the risk avoidance mode lasts so long and is to such an extreme that it is to the detriment of the company. Infrastructure projects are continuously delayed and "under evaluation" seemingly forever. The status quo is "safe" and new technologies, or anything not directly under their control, are suspect. I have been surprised at how often IT teams sabotage new initiatives even though the initiative is in the best interest of the company, but they feel personally threatened by it.

For example, I worked with a fairly large New York City company that had four people on the IT team. One of their team members was a system administrator with more than seventeen years of experience. I was engaged to help them design a new Microsoft Exchange system with disaster recovery built-in. They had half a dozen locations and were planning on opening several more. When I walked into their server room, I was quite surprised to find they had more than a dozen physical servers. The servers themselves were all mid to high level servers and were an investment of more than $100,000. The design wasn't necessarily wrong, but it was odd given the state of virtual technologies. A single physical server can run multiple virtual machines (VMs) and a majority of their machines only had a single application running on it.

As part of our due diligence, we recommended decommissioning some of the older machines and virtualizing some applications to run on the same machine. Our recommendation would save the company money on infrastructure costs and in long-term support costs, but the system administrator fought against the recommendation. He tried to make the argument that virtualization was risky and often failed. The argument was baffling in the face of the current state of the industry. It didn't make technical or business sense. After meeting with him one-on-one it dawned on me that two things were going on. First and foremost, he saw those servers as his job security. The more servers the company had, the more work he could point to in order to justify his job. Second, he had no training or experience with virtualization. He hadn't taken an ongoing training class or certification in nearly a decade and he didn't do much personal study. He had allowed his skill set to expire. He was an expert in ten-year-old technology that was obsolete. It was a dilemma for him and for his company because no one on the management team understood the argument either for or against virtualization.

IT departments stuck in old mindsets do not evolve with the industry. They resist real cost cutting technologies such as cloud services and virtualization and cling to what they know. They are often mired in the tactics of the day-to-day business and fail to think through the strategic applications of technology that would deliver business improvements and efficiencies. And worse, if they do think of an improvement, they are hesitant to make it because failure often equals being fired or replaced.

Over and over again, I see the conundrum damaging businesses. It is persistent and unless stamped out will continue to cause damage for years. The solution to the IT conundrum is an understanding of technology management. As a leader, you don't need to understand the minute details of the work your employees do. Hopefully, they are better at what they do than you are. The most important task of a leader is to understand the right questions to ask to make sure they are on track to delivering the desired result and then give them the right resources to be successful. Chapter 3 will help you begin examining the clues to *Unraveling the Mystery*.

CLUES TO CRACKING THE CODE

●────────────────●

▶ One person cannot handle everything IT over the long haul.

▶ Avoid evaluating performance based on "fighting fires."

▶ Know the right questions to ask to understand the business purpose and risk of a technology issue.

▶ Evaluate your IT team's qualifications: review current certifications, continuing education, and forward thinking.

▶ Is your team qualified to do the work they are doing?

●────────────────●

CHAPTER THREE

•————————•

Unraveling the Mystery

U nraveling the IT conundrum starts with your management team. They must understand how to detect and find the three arch-enemies of IT: cost, down time, and poor productivity. They are the three villains that will oppose you at every turn in your business. Each of them can be defeated for a period of time, but they always seem to find a way to reappear and commit another crime against your business. It is a never-ending struggle. In the next section, I will help you understand how to follow the clues to finding each villain's hide out and how to put together a successful strategy to win the fight.

Step One in IT Management: Understand the Work

Before building your strategy, you must understand the basic work that needs to be done on an ongoing basis, who should do it, and what are the costs. This knowledge will help you keep the villains of IT at bay. It will help you determine what help you will need and who your allies should be to make you successful.

A core misunderstanding of IT management lies in how we think of the technology itself. If a device has electricity flowing through it, then it seems to fall under the umbrella of IT with the expectation that everyone working in IT will know exactly how to troubleshoot and fix it on the spot. But all jobs lumped under the "technology" umbrella are the not same. In fact, in some cases they are completely separate fields of knowledge.

For instance, do you ask your plumber to do your electrical work? Of course not. Plumbing is, well, plumbing. It is unrelated to electrical work. Under the broad category of home construction or home systems they might be related but the similarities end there. And of course your electrician doesn't touch your plumbing. For some reason, in technology, management teams seem to treat all things IT as if they are part of the same discipline. And nothing could be further from the truth.

Take a minute and think about just the different hardware in a business: desktop and laptop computers, smart phones, tablets, servers, switches, firewalls, routers, printers, scanners, fax machines, and many other devices. And now think about all of their variations by manufacturer and within a manufacturer's product line the different models over time. It is a dizzying array of variation. And now think of the vast number of software programs all of your different hardware may employ or interact with in some way. It is not unusual for a single company to use more than one hundred different technologies with dozens of different variations.

The problem is the large variety of technologies makes it impossible to know them all. IT is actually divided into four main categories with many sub-categories of niche expertise. For most companies there are four main disciplines of IT that are needed in a given year. A company may need a sub-category for a limited period of time based on a specific need, but the four main categories cover the vast majority of issues.

The Four Core Disciplines of IT

System Admin	Help Desk Engineer
System Architect	CTO/CIO

In general these are the four Information Technology (IT) disciplines a company will need in a given year. The amount of time needed from an expert will vary from company to company and year to year, but over time all will be needed. An engineer expert in each discipline are the allies you will need to fight the good fight against the three villains.

The top two, system administrator and help desk engineer, are the core of any team. You will need them on nearly a daily basis to keep your network and computers running smoothly and efficiently. They are the guards at the front gate keeping the bandits from raiding your business and stealing your data and wrecking everything you have built. They fight productivity loss by troubleshooting individual problems your team members have over time and they plan the replacement of equipment as it is needed.

The bottom two are more strategic to the business. You may only need their expertise once or twice a year. They are planning the direction of the hardware, software, and connectivity. They are ensuring the goals of the business, budget, and technology are in full alignment. They analyze risk, assume acceptable levels of risk and take precaution against the remaining risk.

There are many other types of technology specialists the company might ally itself with over time in certain areas such as software development, phone systems, ERP, CRM, marketing automation, etc., but they are not addressed individually here. Instead, in chapter 10, I outline how to pick the right technology partner and ally when you need one.

Systems Architect: In this role the company's technological composition is designed to the needs of the company. The various systems of servers, switches, firewalls, routers, etc., are choreographed to provide the company with the data, connectivity, and processing power they need. A systems architect will generally be an experienced engineer with at least some expertise in each of the major devices and brands they manage. They will often have a vendor specific expertise such as Cisco, HP, or SonicWALL.

System Administrator (sysadmin): The system administrator handles the day-to-day maintenance and up-keep of the network. They implement new software patches and virus updates to system equipment, as well as add and remove users to the network, e-mail, and phone system as users enter and depart the company. They usually handle security issues, password protection, and permissions to view company files and folders. They are focused on the software that runs on the devices and not necessarily the devices themselves. The system administrator is an important role and, depending on the size and growth pattern of the organization, can be handled by a journeyman or senior engineer.

Help Desk Engineer: Help desk professionals are the most visible IT professionals. They are the firefighters handling the daily issues of users. They are primarily focused at the individual level: desktop/laptop support and mobile devices. They are generalists who will need working knowledge of the various operating systems of the organization, the e-mail system, basic security, and connectivity issues. Very often help desk engineers are entry level IT professionals with a small number of certifications and experience.

Chief Information Officer (CIO): The CIO is the leader of the IT organization and is primarily responsible for aligning the company's business plan with available technology and resources. They will manage the IT team's daily work and set the strategic direction of the department, budget, new technology selection, and implementation. They are the quarterback calling the plays the team will follow to get the best result for the organization.

In smaller companies of 150 or fewer employees, it is not unusual for all four roles to be filled by a single individual. The difficulty management teams have is that they do not have the budget to hire four different individuals because they do not have enough full-time work to justify the cost. Instead they hire a generalist who does his best to fill every role. And when he becomes overwhelmed, they generally hire another generalist. Without a clear understanding of what skill sets the individual will need to make them successful in the organization it is easy for the management team to hire the wrong person. It is a complex problem and most companies end up wildly understaffing or the pendulum swings in the opposite direction and they overstaff or hire someone for a high-level specialty they need right now but not on an ongoing basis.

Step Two in IT Management: Understand Your Numbers

There are two important numbers every management team must understand in order to make good IT decisions: the company downtime calculation and the cost of delivering IT support. These numbers will help shape all IT related decisions, such as: Should we hire a second person? Should we buy a new server? Is the cost of this cloud service a good buy for us or is it too expensive? The answers to all of these types of questions begin with an understanding of cost structures.

These two numbers will help you right size your IT budget. As a rule of thumb, the less downtime a business can tolerate, the higher the cost; and the inverse is also true, the more downtime a business can absorb, the lower the costs. It is important to understand the right amount of downtime because the difference in cost between a few hours of tolerance and no downtime ever can be thousands of dollars.

What does downtime cost the company?

For our purposes, downtime cost is defined as the cost of a single individual or the entire company to not be "down" or unproductive due to a technology issue. It could be as simple as a single individual who cannot access their e-mail for fifteen minutes to a complex issue that prevents the entire company from working effectively for hours or even days at a time.

To calculate the downtime cost of a single individual, use the burdened cost of a single individual for an entire year and then calculate their cost per hour. To account for taxes, medical benefits, retirement benefits, etc., use 30 percent as a burden rate. Each company may have a slightly different burden rate, but this seems to be a fair approximation for most companies. Calculate this with 1,850 hours of work time a year. It accounts for vacation, sick leave, personal days, days late, etc. Again it is just an approximation and can be customized for an individual case:

Downtime Cost

EC - Employee Compensation
(base+bonus/compensation)

1.3 - Estimated Burden rate
(taxes, medical, 401K, etc.)

1,850 - *Rough number of working hours in a year*

$$\text{Cost per hour} = \frac{(EC \times 1.3)}{1,850 \text{ hrs}}$$

Example:

$60,000 *base salary* + **$10,000** *bonus* = EC of **$70,000**

$$\frac{(\$70,000 \times 1.3 = \$91,000 \text{ Burdened cost})}{1,850 \text{ hrs}} = \$49 \text{ per hour}$$

In this scenario, downtime for employees in this category will cost roughly $50 per hour or $400 a day per employee.

- Adjust downtime calculations to include lost revenue in positions directly related to non-recoverable sales, trading, billable hours, etc.

- Executive estimates are generally three to ten times the employee average; CEOs should be calculated individually.

- Establish employee categories to calculate a company average for company-wide outages.

What is the cost of support?

Calculating the support costs of the company is similar to the cost of downtime calculation, only now we are going to include additional costs: outside consulting, tech support, training, and an estimate of how the support structure might be contributing to downtime.

If we use the same burdened cost rate from our last example:

Employee cost:	$91,000
Outside consulting:	$5,000
Tech Support:	$1,500
Training:	$1,200
Downtime Contribution:	$8,000
	$106,700

In this scenario the company has a support cost run rate of approximately $8,892 per month. Keep in mind this run rate does not include the cost of engaging a CIO or systems architect. This is just the cost to keep the company running.

I calculated the "downtime contribution" based on typical downtime experienced by individuals and a company that is supported by a single individual. Very often this number is much, much higher and is a result of how support is delivered to the company.

Step Three in IT Management: Understand the Skills

As I mentioned before, there are two types of ongoing work in a typical company: personnel support and network support. The two buckets of work mainly fall under systems administration and help desk support. The two roles are interrelated but they are very different skill sets. Understanding the two basic roles will help you look for clues toward reducing costs and finding productivity accelerators.

The Main Tasks of the System Administrator:

- Security updates
- Software patches
- Add and remove users from the system
- Reset passwords
- Maintain and analyze network logs
- Install new software
- Data Backups
- New equipment installation
- Document all changes

The Main Tasks of Help Desk:

- Desktop/Laptop Support
- Mobile Device Support
- Email Support
- Internet Support
- Ticket management
- Reporting
- Trend analysis

In very large companies the work of a system administrator may even be segmented into more discrete tasks such as security administrator, network administrator, backup administrator, etc. These are just some of the top-level main tasks that should be reviewed with the management team in most companies. There are many sub-tasks, but trying to manage and monitor them all is not necessary. What is essential is to understand the differences between systems administration and help desk support.

Step Four in IT Management: Collect Information

Now that you have a basic understanding of the underlying issues, you can begin to build your IT strategy. It is a straightforward process:

1. Inventory all of your hardware and software and note the purchase date, warranty status, version, and license renewal date as applicable.

2. Track all of your help desk requests for one month. Note the total time they take to resolve and create an estimate of downtime per individual.

3. Document all systems administration tasks separate from the help desk requests.

If you already have a solid ticketing system and well-documented department you may already have all of the information at your fingertips. Or you may have to start from scratch. It is not unusual for a company, as troubling as it might seem, to have no documentation whatsoever. No ticketing system. No hardware, software, or warranty information. And no documentation that any of your networks devices have ever been patched, updated, or backed up in anyway.

With your new found understanding of the conundrum—your numbers, roles, the tasks to be done, and the current state of your company—you are ready to start following the clues that lead to a balanced IT strategy. You never want any of the three villains to gain an advantage on your company. Costs can be controlled with proper planning, downtime can be thoughtfully managed, and productivity will only improve with more efficient use of the technology you already have or may purchase and implement in the future. Now that you have a basic foundation of understanding the work to be done and the questions to ask it is time to look for savings. The next chapter will help you find the *Clues to Cost Savings.*

CLUES TO CRACKING THE CODE

▶ What are your downtime numbers?

▶ What is your cost of support?

▶ How are you currently receiving support for the four roles of IT?

▶ What system administration tasks are currently *not* being addressed in your business?

CHAPTER FOUR

—————•—————

Clues to Cost Savings

M ost companies start with the question, how do I lower costs? But what if you were already in cost saving mode and were underspending on IT? Then the question can lead to disaster as lowering costs further can increase the risk of downtime, cause a security issue, or lead you to miss a key productivity increase that could be strategic to the company.

The first question to ask is, how much should we be spending on IT? There is no right or wrong answer. The answer of what you should be spending is dependent on information you gathered in chapter 3. It will vary by company based on their ability to absorb downtime and the age and complexity of their infrastructure.

IT support costs are primarily driven by the complexity of the environment, who is supporting it, the number of computers, data backup, and the amount of variation within the environment. If you can improve the performance of the company in any of these areas, you can usually reduce costs.

One of the most common culprits driving support costs is complexity. They have not standardized or updated old equipment and day-to-day problems take an enormous amount of manual labor to troubleshoot and keep running. Not understanding the core problem, managers often hire to treat the symptoms rather than treating the core issue that they need to invest in infrastructure standardization. By spending more on infrastructure they can many times actually reduce overall costs including downtime and support costs.

Standardization saves money by saving service time. By removing complexity from the IT environment, it becomes enormously easier to support as a system. The points of failure become more obvious and easier to repair in the event of a problem. Troubleshooting a problem and trying to understand what and how it is occurring is often the most expensive portion of a problem.

While a captain in the US Army in charge of the maintenance program of a mechanized infantry battalion, one of the most difficult part of the job was not identifying problems or even having the resources to address them. The real difficulty was in understanding what to do about them when they occurred. Some of the problems were extremely complex. When a tank has an engine problem, which is literally the same engine as a jet, it can be an ordeal to find out exactly what is wrong. The army has invested millions of dollars in diagnostic equipment, repair manuals, and training to make troubleshooting easier but they have hardly touched the main issue.

The core of the problem is complexity. Every vehicle in the battalion had a parts list, but among models the list is different. Sometimes the exact same model of vehicle could have the same parts list but from a different manufacturer who had introduced different modifications because at the time of the order there was a need. The result was parts that were incompatible or parts that were exactly the same but had different part numbers and names and therefore were very difficult to identify.

The experience taught me a vital lesson that directly applies to IT—the seams where systems touch each other are where much of the failure will occur. In the mechanized infantry, the seams were where the thermal optics connected to the gun or the communication system interacted with the GPS. In IT, much of your failure will occur when you integrate multiple systems together such as Google with Microsoft.

So how can you tell if you need to spend more or less?

COST SAVINGS CLUE: **Standardize and Manage Lifecycles**

By replacing hardware on a schedule you will reduce your overall long term support costs while reducing the risk of extended downtime and loss of productivity. Below is a very general guideline I use to help plan the life cycle.

**Hardware Lifetime
Rules of Thumb:**

Desktops:	*3-5 years*
Laptops:	*2-3 years*
Servers:	*3-4 years*
Switches, routers, wireless devices:	*4-5 years*

The rule of thumb is not a law. Of course there are always outliers. You will have equipment that fails well within the time period and some that lasts far longer. I have a laptop at my house right now that I have had for seven awesome years of use and counting. But I don't travel with it, I understand its limitations, and I have the data on it backed up. I think of it as a ticking time bomb. At some point it will have a catastrophic failure.

What you should be focused on are the averages. The outliers are what cause owners to make the mistake of thinking they should wait until failure of everything rather than making deliberate updates. Remember, the older the equipment the more difficult it is to support because of changes in software and security.

Also, not all hardware is created equal. Some vendors build better products than others with the mean time between failures being significantly lower and usually better daily performance.

The cost of the warranty leaves a clue to failure rates as compared to prices. Companies have a good understanding of the average failure rates of their equipment and normally the higher the cost of the warranty for two like products the more likely the product is to fail within a set period of time. If you paid relatively little for your warranties and the equipment is on the outer edges of the rule of thumb than you should start planning for its immediate replacement.

Once you understand what needs to be replaced, pick a standard. Having a standard, *almost any standard*, may be more important than which vendor you actually choose! Choose one operating system and vendor and migrate everyone there as soon as possible. It will help defeat all three villains almost immediately.

COST SAVINGS CLUE: Manage Your Backups

Over the course of time, the average business generates an enormous amount of information that they need to store, manage, and backup. As the amount of data grows the cost of storage and maintenance of the backups grow with it. In recent years many companies moved from tape backup to online backup providers. One drawback of cloud backup is the pricing model. Depending on the service, you generally will pay for the amount of storage, the delta change over a given period of time, and recovery time or how long it will take to recover information when needed.

Careful management of the data you backup can save an enormous amount of money. With the loosening of IT rules at many companies and the entire Bring Your Own Device (BYOD) revolution, companies are often surprised to find out they are paying to store gigs or even hundreds of gigs of employee's music and video files that were uploaded on company equipment. Careful management of the actual types of media that are stored and backed up can save businesses thousands of dollars a year.

The next area of savings in backup management is archiving. The longer a company is in business, the less likely they are to access older files. Many of the more advanced backup services have the ability to move data into an inactive archive and the storage cost is often deeply discounted as "static" data. For instance you can run an analysis of all files more than three years old and if they have not been accessed for more than a year move them to the archive.

And finally, the total amount of data that is stored and managed can be reduced by removing duplicates of files. For instance, if a file is sent to everyone in the company, it is easy in an unmanaged environment for that file to be backed up for each individual! In an advanced backup system, it will remove duplicates and store a single instance of the file and remember where each copy of it was placed. This one simple change can save thousands of dollars by dramatically reducing the amount of data that needs to be backed up.

If you are able to determine that older data will not likely be needed again, but you want to keep a copy just in case, it might even be worthwhile to archive it to a small portable hard drive and store it locally or in a safe deposit box and removed from the active cloud storage. A small drive can hold two to four TB of data and costs a couple of hundred dollars. It is a very cost effective way to save.

COST SAVINGS CLUE: **Who Does the Work Matters**

One of the best ways to save money in IT is to change who does the work. Unfortunately, for most companies with fewer than 200 people, a single person cannot usually handle the volume or complexity of the work. There is just too much to know and too few hours in the day to handle all of the issues well.

As we discussed in chapters 2 and 3, it is nearly impossible for any one person to wear every hat that is needed in a company. It is not efficient or cost effective to try. In order to see if you are a good candidate for outsourcing all or a portion of your IT to a partner try this litmus test.

Imagine your IT department as a standalone company. Take the monthly run rate you calculated for your company in chapter 3 (in the example I used it was $8,892/month), and approach three Managed IT providers and ask for proposals for service. Compare the service they can provide at that rate and compare it to the service you get from your department. For companies from fifteen to two hundred seats, more likely than not, the Managed IT provider will be more cost effective. Use chapter 10—the outsourcing guide—to help you in choosing the right partner.

Spending the right amount on IT is important, but buying the right technology that supports the business plan may be even more vital to the health of an organization. In the next couple of chapters we will examine the clues that lead to business improvements that are enabled by the intelligent application of the right technology, especially the cloud in *Unlocking the Cloud*.

CLUES TO CRACKING THE CODE

▶ Reduce complexity as much as practical: create company standards and implement them over time.

▶ Schedule and budget for hardware and software refreshes. They will save on support soft costs over the long-term.

▶ Review in detail your backup plan—eliminate unnecessary data and archive old, unused data.

▶ Are qualified technologists doing the right work?

▶ Get comparison quotes from vendors using your support cost numbers from Chapter 3.

CHAPTER FIVE

•————————•

Unlocking the Cloud

"The pace of change of our human-created technology is accelerating and its powers are expanding at an exponential pace."
—RAY KURZWEIL, *THE SINGULARITY IS NEAR*

Cloud computing is possibly one of the most overly hyped terms of the twenty-first century. It is also a place with the potential of decreasing costs and downtime, while increasing productivity. Any analysis of your IT plan would be remiss if it didn't include consideration of the cloud.

The cloud is not just one technology. It is the convergence of software, hardware, and connectivity. Fast bandwidth allows companies to sell computing power and the power of software in a way that did not exist before. It can allow a company to pay for this power on a monthly basis rather than buying it all up front and managing it themselves. It is a new type of outsourcing. Rather than outsourcing labor alone, it is outsourcing technology too. Technology outsourcing is the next evolutionary step in business and currently it is possible with nearly all technology: hardware, software, telephony, computing power, and data storage.

But beware. The technology is still maturing. Before you throw your entire business into the cloud you need to understand your new numbers, the basics of buying a cloud service, and how it may affect your battle with the three villains: cost, downtime, and poor productivity.

The first place to look for a clue to help decide if you will buy a cloud service is the cost structure. Contrary to the message of many marketers, the cloud will not always save your company money. The basic premise of most cloud services is that instead of buying a technology you can subscribe or rent it on a monthly basis. For example let's use a Software as a Service (SaaS) application. Let's say the service is fifty dollars per user per month. That price will usually include not only the software but patches, updates, and security. It also will include some sort of up time guarantee and it will be accessible from virtually any computer with connectivity.

Looking back at your support cost structure, downtime tolerance and budget, you will know quickly if the cost makes sense for you. Is the cost of purchasing and supporting the application far higher than the three to four year cost of subscribing to it? Another consideration and a real advantage of some SaaS platforms are third party applications you can purchase and integrate into the base product. They can help you customize the application without you having to pay the development costs.

Putting hardware in the cloud, primarily servers and phone systems is a little more complicated of a process (see chapter 11). Cost is also the first clue to examine but the comparison is different. Now you will compare the purchase of the equipment with the right software to run it and the support costs over time. Applying the hardware rules of thumb, I usually use four years as the comparison. For a server you have to look at four main costs: CPUs, storage, bandwidth, and support. For some services, if it is a private "cloud" you may also need to buy a firewall to secure it and own licenses to a program to allow you and your team access to it securely. For public services, all of these costs are usually bundled into the subscription fee.

For hardware there are also some performance considerations. The sped of your local bandwidth can greatly affect the user experience of working on a remotely hosted server. You need a broadband connection that is large enough that it can support all of your users at peak times without it running slowly. For many professional services companies who work directly on their servers throughout the day, putting their file server in the cloud is often a mistake. The user experience can be frustrating and it is one instance when the cloud actually reduces productivity.

After examining the cost structures, the next clue to look at may be one of the least obvious—examine the exit strategy from the service. Ask the question, "If we start this service and need to leave for any reason, how will we accomplish it and approximately what will it cost?" The reason you want the answer to the question speaks to the immaturity of the industry. Few companies providing cloud services have a long track record and many "cloud" companies go out of business every year. If they don't go out of business, they may be acquired and the service changed. Or maybe the service is great at first, but as the business grows, it degrades over time. The bottom line is you need to know the exit strategy in advance.

Choose a Side

Large public clouds have developed a real following the last few years. Google, Amazon, IBM, Microsoft, Salesforce, Rackspace, and many others built unique platforms you can use. They are all established businesses with a lower chance of going out of business than some of their smaller competitors.

Choosing the right provider for your company will come down to many factors and ultimately a personal choice, but there is a philosophical issue to keep in mind. You must choose one provider. It is a mistake to try and use more than one provider at the same time.

For instance, in recent years many companies started to migrate to Google's Gmail because of the low cost and good functionality of Gmail. But they continued to use Microsoft Outlook on the desktop. Outlook has become somewhat of a business standard. It is the e-mail client that most people are used to using. Many people have designed entire workflows around it. In January of 2012, Google announced they will no longer support Outlook synchronization. It is the shot across the bow against users trying to use two major providers simultaneously. Now these companies have a small project that needs a solution. They need to choose to either leave Gmail, work directly in Gmail through a browser all the time, or find a supported client that has a workflow that has enough of the functionality of Outlook. Regardless of the solution, it is a headache. The right decision was to move away from Outlook when they chose Gmail in the first place.

Imagine the level of technician needed to trouble shoot the following two environments.

Scenario One

The marketing department's four Mac users are all on different versions of the Mac IOS and the Microsoft users in the company are using a combination of Windows XP, Window 7, and the newest version, Windows 8. All of these users might be uploading files to a file server running ten-year-old software onto a five-year-old server near capacity.

Scenario Two

In Scenario Two, the number of potential problems is greatly reduced and the environment is cheaper to support due to the lower complexity. When a problem occurs, understanding the problem is much easier. The total number of issues that can occur is far fewer than in the first example.

There is absolutely no incentive for Google or Microsoft to cooperate in making their products seamlessly integrate. In fact they have somewhat of an incentive for the integrations not to work right and force customers to choose one side or the other.

Timing Your Move to the Cloud

When is the right time to migrate to the cloud? Most businesses evaluate the cloud when a hardware or software system comes up for an upgrade, reaches end of life, or when planning an office move. These are the times when the cost structure will most often make sense.

Another time to move to the cloud is when you need to add a capability to the company that you don't currently have and do not have a current cost to compare it with. If you do not have sunk cost considerations, very often the ease of starting fresh on a cloud service is lower than the start up from scratch project. Remember, the 3rd villain of IT management is poor productivity and any activity outside of your core business is a distraction. It is difficult to put a price on this as a soft cost, but after working on dozens of projects over time, experience says it is much cheaper in the long run.

The cloud is not just about cost savings. It has the ability to open up entire ecosystems of new technologies and make them available to businesses with no additional infrastructure costs. The powerful capabilities of integrating multiple platforms can revolutionize your business. Next, we will examine the *Technology Secrets of Service*.

CLUES TO CRACKING THE CODE

●────────────────●

▶ Choose a platform and go all in with the provider.

▶ Choose a provider with mainstream acceptance and an ecosystem of developers around it.

▶ Do the ROI calculation of cloud versus premise equipment and software before making new purchases.

●────────────────●

CHAPTER SIX

• ━━━━━━━━━━━ •

The Technology Secret of Service

"When your organization becomes more human, more remarkable, faster on its feet, and more likely to connect directly with customers, it becomes indispensable."

—SETH GODIN, *LINCHPIN*

My wife Tanya shops at the grocery store Trader Joe's. Trader Joe's is not the cheapest place in town. They sell unique, healthy food that is difficult to find anywhere else. It is a hip store to shop at and more environmentally conscious than most. But none of those are the reason she is there—she is there for the balloons.

She usually shops with my two sons, Danya and Andrey. They are generally good boys, and like all boys they are incredibly energetic and have selective hearing. Tanya takes them to Trader Joe's because they give away free helium balloons in a multitude of colors. They also frequently have small samples the kids can try, which are almost always kid friendly and tasty.

When you are two, or even five years old, balloons are a big deal. Kids will help momma at the store for a balloon. They will keep their hands in their pockets for a balloon. Balloons transform shopping with two small boys from a hair pulling experience into something to somewhat enjoy. Trader Joe's gets it. The human connection of a smiling woman giving two excited boys balloons is pure genius.

Connection makes sales. Something as simple and thoughtful as a couple of balloons motivates Tanya to drive an extra twenty minutes out of her way to spend her hard earned money. And we wouldn't have it any other way.

The urge to do business with people we know and like is ingrained in the human race. We are social beings at heart. We are very much herd animals who want to run together, live together, and know each other. That is one of the reasons "social media" is so sticky. Intimate contact with our herd is fun and emotionally satisfying.

The Internet is changing who is in our herd, what makes a neighbor a neighbor, and how we connect with one another. And it is expanding who we can do business with far beyond what was once thought of as the normal reach of a business.

For thousands of years, humans lived in small villages and towns in which everyone knew everyone—and they knew nearly everything about one another too. Gossip was news. In ancient times, the "town crier" was an actual career whose responsibility was to pass on the news of the day. As the world grew, cities sprung up creating huge mobs of people where knowing everyone was no longer possible. The village concept was supplanted by neighborhoods.

We want to do business with people we know and trust. We want to do business within our herd and add new members to our herd whenever possible. People do business with much less regard for distance than ever before. Ask yourself, is the Internet local? How about Google? Google provides a free search service to millions of people every day, but are they local to you?

Imagine for a moment you call your accountant to ask them a question. Does how far away they are from you make a difference? Most likely they are fairly local, but that is not as necessary as it once was. In today's networked world Rochester, New York is as local to Idaho Falls as Boise, Idaho. They are both just a phone call away. Documents can be exchanged via e-mail or fax in an instant. Video conferencing can be done between you and your accountant at a very low cost or even for free. We want to have relationships with people we know and trust—and that is who we want to do business with—no matter where they are geographically located.

The Trader Joe's example is inarguably low tech but the analogy is clear. Connection and the wow factor are the keys to building relationships that last a life time. Another good example is Zappos. They use a high tech call center to deliver what is little more than personalized, amazing service. Each representative is given the flexibility to connect with customers in small ways. To create a wow factor that cannot be scripted.

The new economy has several characteristics. Increased competition and choice means people are looking for entertainment and engagement; good service is often more important than being the lowest cost vendor. If you are in what is thought to be strictly a commodity business, such as the grocery business, then service may be your only substantial competitive advantage. Keep in mind why my family shops at Trader Joe's— for the amazing food *and* service. The price is third in our evaluation criteria.

No doubt, providing great customer service costs more. The benefit is happier customers. Customers who feel connected and valued. Customers who are delighted by your service will keep coming back and they will spread the word of your product or service in ways you may not imagine.

Technology can help your customer service reps become more human to your customers and build real connections. One example is to connect a Customer Relationship Management (CRM) system to a smart telephone system. By connecting the two, representatives will know who is calling before they pick up the phone. If done correctly, they can receive screen pops with a customer's full information and account activity. If you keep the database up to date, your representatives will understand more about your customers than just about any of your competitors.

The data collection doesn't have to be manual and difficult. By integrating your CRM system with the phone system, much of the data collection will be automated. Each call can query the database and pull up your customer's information automatically and append a recording of the call or a log of the call with the representative's notes.

If an inbound number is not currently in the system, your representative can quickly find the customer's record and link the new number to the record so that the next inbound call generates the correct record. One call at a time, your team will build a profile on each customer that will last a lifetime. Start to build the relationship with the customers.

In the old economy, companies tried to provide the minimum level of service necessary to keep the customer from complaining. There were few choices and companies could get away with fifteen to twenty minute wait times in call center queues. If you have called just about any monopoly business today, such as your power company or large wireless phone provider, you know what I mean. They don't have to provide you with good service. No matter how frustrated and annoyed you are with their poor service, there is nothing you can do about it. Your power company knows that if you want electricity, you have to get it from them (yes, you could figure out a way to go off grid, but for most people this is not a viable option).

The e-mail below is a real e-mail I received from Connecticut Light and Power. After calling them for three straight days and hanging up after the queue told me it would be a forty-seven minute wait time, I tried their online e-mail address. My somewhat annoyed e-mail and their response is below.

From: Anthony Butler <xyz@hotmail.com>

To: talktous@nu.com

40-45 minute wait time! It has been like this for going on 3 days.
Ridiculous.

To: Anthony Butler <xyz@hotmail.com>

From: talktous@nu.com

Subject: RE: ***Connecticut Light and Power Automated Email Responder***

Connecticut Light & Power

Thank you for your recent email.

We apologize for the long hold time in responding to your phone call. It is sometimes necessary for customers to be placed on hold. We make every attempt to minimize this inconvenience.

Please use our Moving Wizard to process a move request at the link below:

http://www.cl-p.com/home/customerservice/moving.aspx

Thank you for your interest in our web site. We hope you will find it easy to use and beneficial in answering questions and concerns relating to your account. Please contact us at www.cl-p.com if you need further assistance.

I tried the moving wizard and of course it didn't work. It would not allow me to start new service unless I agreed to turn off service at another location. Of course I just wanted to turn on new service. I felt cheated. The representative sent me a worthless link because there was no communication and she didn't know what I needed.

I was so angry I wasted a solid hour researching ways to get off the grid before I finally bit the bullet and waited them out for *fifty-three minutes on hold*. If I had realized the first couple of times I called that a forty-seven minute wait time was a good deal, I would have stayed on longer. I finally got a very nice, albeit somewhat overwhelmed, woman on the phone to help me and it was smooth sailing from there.

The customer service debacle described above was just a precursor to what occurred in the late summer and fall of 2011. CL & P experienced two natural disasters that knocked out service to hundreds of thousands of clients for as long as two weeks. They were poorly prepared for either disaster and their service during the disasters was non-existent. It was a showcase in incompetence.

CL&P can get away with such poor service because they know there is nothing I can do. I am a captive customer—a hostage to the lack of choice. Some bureaucrat at CL&P figured out it was profitable to extend wait times to just below the threshold that might launch a government investigation and avoid a consumer lawsuit. Lowering wait times costs money and since they have a veritable monopoly they don't care about me or any of their customers for that matter. They know they are going to get my money because I need electricity and they are the only game in town providing it.

| Big Company | + | Hostage Customer Base | = | Poor Service Every Time |

If your business is like most businesses and it is in a competitive market, then poor service as I described above is not an option. In competitive markets, the experience is everything. If you are in a commodity business, experience may be the *only* difference between you and the competition. Customers have a choice and they will leave you for better service. Customer loyalty, if it exists at all, is extremely short lived.

Most companies spend enormous sums to gain a new customer. For many companies acquiring a new customer is one of the most expensive parts of their business. Profits are found in repeat customers. Repeat customers are more profitable than new customers because now the original acquisition cost is spread over multiple purchases. If you do a good job the first time and establish some sort of relationship, chances are the customer will buy from you again. A one-time transaction with a customer may not cover the extra costs of employing extraordinary people, but when you are able to calculate the lifetime value of a customer who becomes a repeat buyer over time, the numbers change dramatically. If you keep them happy they will keep coming back again and again. There is magic in customers who stay with you for two years, three years, or more than ten years.

Two Businesses—One Difference

Imagine for a moment two competing businesses in the same city. Their owners went to school together and built identical businesses. They both offer a great product with good service. They both have competent, well-trained sales teams.

But one owner subscribes to a hosted voice service and integrates it with his CRM system, e-mail, and marketing automation software. His plan is to capture as much of his customer interactions as possible and to empower his customer service representatives to solve problems in a more intimate way. He also hires customer service representatives in multiple time zones. They work from independent home offices using remote work tools and answer calls live twenty-four hours a day, seven days a week.

He realizes that in troubled times, he needs real information about his service and customers. He needs to focus his entire attention on the core business. Anything outside of the core business is a distraction—a waste of time, energy, and focus. To take his company to the next level he needs an improvement in his technology while avoiding the cost of buying, implementing, and running the system himself. He knows many large, well-known companies are using the service, but he feels even better knowing hundreds of other small business owners looking for an edge in their business are subscribing to the same service.

Using his new service he begins to uncover business breakthroughs. He tracks his call logs for thirty days and realizes Tuesdays call volume is low and he is overstaffed and during certain peak hours customers are not getting through. He adds a queue and rearranges staffing schedules to increase customer service. He sets a goal for every call to be answered in two minutes or less.

His system integrates with his CRM software and his sales team exponentially increases their use of CRM providing his sales manager with leading indicators of performance. From real data he is able to discern that one of his lead sources is time consuming and has an extremely low conversion rate. He eliminates it and refocuses the team's efforts on higher quality leads.

He uses his marketing engine to capture exactly which advertisements are producing quality leads and calculates the exact marketing ROI or each advertisement. By eliminating poor performing ads he saves 30 percent of his advertising budget without reducing his lead flow.

At the end of the year, the first owner who invested in technology increased revenues by 40 percent while decreasing marketing costs. The competing owner increased revenues by a respectable, but far less, 12 percent, and he will need to invest more in the future in order to attempt to catch up to the competition.

The first owner's choice to leverage technology not only paid for itself the first year, it dramatically improved business performance. Most importantly, it increased the profitability of the business because customers were better served.

The difference? The high performing business aligned their technology with their business plan. They thoughtfully selected hardware and software and got expert help integrating it. Technology is a tool managers need to help them understand how to improve service. It helps them analyze and understand what the customer experience is when they call. Technology helps managers determine who their best service employees are and how to help make them even better.

Managers need to understand deeply how their employees are doing so they can adjust. You should ask yourself a few questions about your manager's ability to monitor and improve customer interactions. Are they monitoring live calls? Where are they capturing customer data? Are they able to record calls for training purposes? Are they conducting on-going training to help their teams handle the most difficult calls? If the answer to any of the above is an emphatic "No!" then it is time to invest in better technology.

Measurement Improves Customer Service

Service related businesses that improve the experience of customers can improve the bottom line. The difficulty often lies in determining what to measure and how to measure it accurately on a day-to-day basis. Meaningful metrics tell an important story about individual employee performance and the habits and needs of customers.

The first question to ask is, "What is the customer's experience when they call or e-mail?" To get to the heart of this of course requires other questions, such as:

- How long did they wait until someone answered?

- What was the result?

- Are my customer service representatives polite, helpful, and well-trained?

Chances are you have a gut feel for the answer to each question. But how do you really know if you do not have a way to monitor and measure the answer to each question. Business owners are often astounded at the real answers to these questions when they first start measuring service.

Application integration is a business differentiator. It creates competitive leverage for businesses looking for an edge. In the early years of the twentieth century, punch cards were the largest application that helped businesses innovate. Companies that were able to deploy punch card systems early gained a distinct advantage over their competitors. Following innovations in punch cards came rented computing time on main frames, personal computers, and now hosted applications that allow businesses to easily customize and integrate applications that fit their needs.

In order to choose the right tools from all available technologies and align the business plan and budget requires a technologist who is also business savvy. They must understand what is possible technologically, the resources required, and the business impact. If you have this person on staff already then you are very lucky, but more likely than not this person is not on your staff. Few in-house technologists have broad enough technological and business experience to help and it will require partnering with an outside expert.

Now that you have some new ideas on how technology can improve your service you are ready to examine the most powerful game changing integrations that most companies didn't even know are possible. Next we will examine the *Technology Clues to Improve Sales and Marketing.*

CLUES TO CRACKING THE CODE

▶ Look for ways to integrate systems to improve service: CRM, e-mail, marketing, telephony, analytics, etc.

▶ Periodically look for Apps that can be easily integrated into your current systems to improve service.

▶ Gather data about your service and share it with sales, marketing, and operations.

CHAPTER SEVEN

•————————•

Cracking Customer Relationships and Marketing Automation

"Half the money I spend on advertising is wasted; the trouble is, I don't know which half."

—John Wanamaker

Sales managers have one of the most difficult jobs. They must lead a team of often quirky and difficult sales people, as well as sift through a mountain of information to try and forecast the sales numbers months and quarters in advance.

During a current month they are often pulling their hair out trying to get sales people to enter critical data into a CRM system so they have up to date information. Top sales reps push back with, "Why should I waste time putting information in CRM? I made my number." Reps that are not making their numbers push back with, "I need to spend my time with prospects and not endlessly updating CRM."

Even the poorest excuses come with a grain of truth. Manually inputting information into a CRM is a waste of time. It does take too long. Most reps will track information offline in their own system—be it paper, Outlook, or Excel—and then come back later and enter some of it into their company's CRM system. For most reps, productivity decreases when they begin using CRM, as they enter data twice and the data they enter is often sparse, outdated, and of questionable accuracy.

Selling is transactional and time management is absolutely critical. Professionals carefully guard their time against intrusion and unnecessary bureaucracy. Paperwork is the bane of sales professionals, and in some cases one of the most time consuming tasks is keeping the CRM system properly up to date.

Integration of a phone system, CRM system, e-mail, and marketing software can revolutionize a sales organization. All calls can be made click to dial from an interface and data auto-captured with wrap up codes. The sales reps don't have to do anything extra. In fact it saves them a dramatic amount of time. Sales people who become power users of their tools become power sellers.

Here are some reasons that integration is more efficient:

- It can decrease dial times by twenty to thirty seconds per call. In high dial businesses such as an outbound sales team this can add up to an hour or more per sales rep per day.

- Capturing meaningful data becomes much easier. Every call is captured live in the system without additional human interaction needed. Activity reports can be run hourly, daily, weekly, etc.

- Understanding the activity of outside reps becomes much easier. When in the office they make all calls through the system and it leaves them only with outside correspondence to put into the system.

- Wrap up codes can be used to categorize each call. The wrap up codes can be analyzed to understand more about the nature of each call. In many environments inside sales teams are both making and receiving a variety of calls and understanding where they are spending the majority of their time can create critical data that changes the business plan.

- Once the data in a CRM system becomes more up to date and easier to keep fresh, sales reps realize the system is not just a way for the company to watch over them. It becomes a tool that can help them earn more money because they can handle a much larger amount of inbound and outbound correspondence than can someone not using an integrated CRM system.

Marketing's Waste Factor

The world of marketing is ripe with waste. It is the one department that CFOs and CEOs allow to function, often times, with little tangible results—or worse, getting good results without a deep understanding of what is working and why. Decent results actually increase the waste factor in marketing. Because much of the marketing of a company goes unmeasured and not linked to a specific ROI, if the aggregate results are decent, then there is rarely a deep dissection of the marketing to determine what is working. Direct mail, catalogs, trade shows, and newspaper and magazine advertisements are repeated for months or even years with no valid proof they are even paying for themselves. Small to mid-sized businesses routinely spend tens of thousands of dollars on marketing while attributing sales success to the program without it ever being measured.

For instance, a company may send out three or four different direct mail advertisements simultaneously. If hypothetically the combined campaigns increase lead flow by 3 percent the program is a success. But what if one of the campaigns actually failed? Wouldn't it be more efficient to know the results of each campaign? The poor performing campaign could be improved or eliminated and the marketing budget reinvested in the campaigns that are working. The key is to precisely track the response rates of each program separately. One method would be to run each program in sequence and allow for results to be tallied against each other over a period time.

A better way to track marketing spend is to isolate the response of each piece of advertising and link it to generated leads and ultimately new sales. One of the easiest ways to conduct the test is a using the "call through" method. Working similarly to how Google Ad Words™ works where individual "click-throughs" are tracked to a specific landing page and then to an order form, "call-throughs" are tracked by assigning a unique phone number to every single advertisement that is sent out. The phone number acts like a license plate number that can be traced back to the make and model of an individual car, but in this case, an individual piece of advertising.

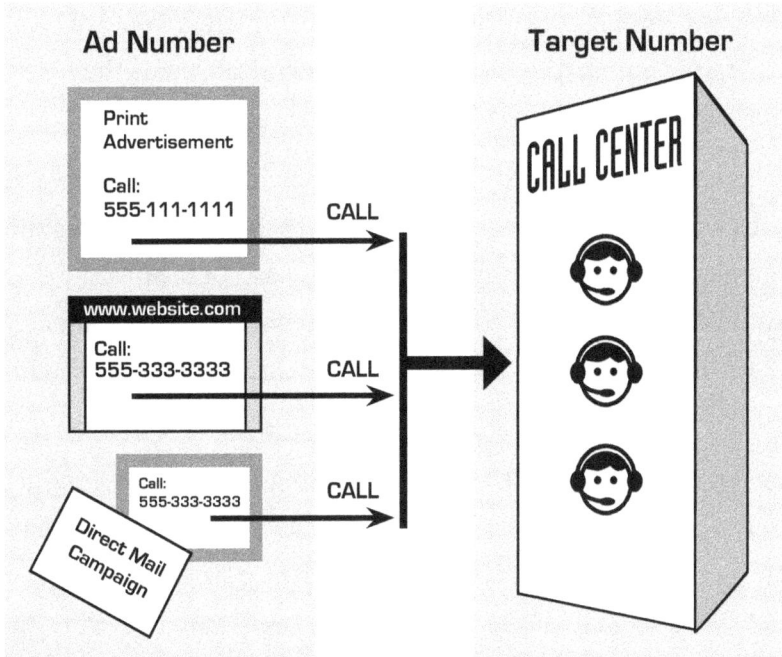

The Ad number can point to any target number and answered seamlessly. A target number can have multiple Ad numbers pointed to it. The Ad numbers and target numbers do not matter to the caller.

People like to do business locally. If thoughtfully planned and executed, each advertised number will be local to the potential customer even if the target number it is pinned to is long distance.

Local numbers increase response rates. During a radio campaign, a local number will often outperform an 800 number.

For example, imagine a New York company that wants to break into the California market. It might choose a group of numbers clustered around major metropolitan areas such as Los Angeles, San Francisco, and Sacramento. The numbers are local California numbers, but when customers call them they ring into New York or wherever the call center is located.

The magic of this system is that tracking the results of each call becomes simple. Each call is linked to the campaign with the phone number that was published on it. Most of the major CRM systems on the market allow easy phone system integration and these inbound call logs can be populated directly into the system.

At the end of the reporting period, a week or a month, real business intelligence is available. Shifting back to our original four advertisements, the data may tell me that although we had an overall 3 percent response rate, maybe ad number two did not perform well and had a .05 percent response rate with the success of the other ads carrying the majority of the success. A smart manager will then be able to discontinue or revise the underperforming advertisement.

Marketing Automation Systems

Back in the old days, cutting down a redwood tree by hand with an axes and hand saws was a big job—entire teams of lumberjacks would attack a single tree for hours at a time until they could chip away enough wood to finally bring the giant crashing to earth. After the invention of the chain saw an enormous redwood could be brought to earth in a fraction of the time. Marketing has undergone much the same transformation. The chainsaw in this case is marketing automation software. With the explosion of social media and online advertising, marketing has become more complicated than ever. Have you ever tried to track and report results across e-mail, Twitter, LinkedIn, Google+, YouTube, and Facebook simultaneously? How about planning, producing, editing, scheduling, and publishing five to ten different pieces a week? It can easily become an operational nightmare. And if you mix in older media advertising such as direct mail, billboards, magazines, newspapers, television, and radio, it can quickly become unmanageable for a single individual or even a small team.

Marketing automation systems simplify the entire process. They allow a single individual to manage the process in a thoughtful way. The leading systems directly integrate with each type of social media via a portal and allow posts to be scheduled in advance on approval. They automatically track engagement and views through built-in analytics. Offline activities are added through campaign updates and can be done in mass.

Trigger based activities are a powerful way of using the systems. For example, a prospect downloads a whitepaper from a website to get more information and they leave their name, e-mail, and company name. If the marketing automation system is integrated with the CRM system, which all of the top systems allow, it will auto populate the new lead into the CRM and open tasks for the sales team to follow up on. There is no human intervention included until the most crucial moment when they know the prospect is actively thinking about their solution. It can be a game-changing process.

System integration is a business differentiator that can help businesses scale for a fraction of the cost of even three years ago. It helps lower costs by identifying and eliminating poor performing marketing and increases the productivity of sales teams by giving them tools that help them scale their activities.

In the next chapter we examine one of the fastest growing trends in the business world. A trend that generation Y is embracing in droves. We will examine the clues that lead to the technology mix that enables teams to work together from anywhere in the world—*The Remote Work Puzzle.*

CLUES TO CRACKING THE CODE

▶ Choose a CRM and marketing automation system.

▶ Integrate your CRM, e-mail, phone, and marketing automation systems.

▶ Look for platform applications that increase productivity such as online expense reports, e-signatures, digital document libraries, etc.

CHAPTER EIGHT

●————————————●

The Remote Work Puzzle

"There is strong evidence that allowing some people to work from outside the office improves employee morale and retention, reduces costs, increases productivity and even provides benefits beyond the enterprise like reducing traffic and minimizing carbon emissions."
—DAN HOFFMAN

Companies are just starting to understand the many benefits of implementing the technology needed to successfully run a remote work program. According to statistics from the American Community Survey, telecommuters now make up 2.6 percent of the American work force, or 3.2 million workers, and up to 40 million workers are working at home at least part of the time. Though estimates vary, it is clear that these numbers are increasing rapidly.

There are many business advantages of remote work. Some of the advantages are easy to measure, like incorporating remote work into a disaster recovery plan, while other advantages are intangibles, like employee satisfaction and helping employees create a better life work balance. Remote work can also be a great recruiting tool. It has real appeal to Generation Y and may be seen as a reward from other demographics in the workplace. Regardless of the reasons a business implements remote work, technology is the enabler and it must be managed in a thoughtful and deliberate manner to prevent serious issues from developing.

As I will cover in depth in chapter 9, *Cracking Disaster Recovery*, remote work is a key component in the planning of how to stay in business during disasters such as pandemics like the swine flu and Ebola outbreaks, energy shortages, and even terrorist attacks like September 11. There are many other more subtle advantages and few disadvantages.

One of the biggest and most obvious advantages of remote work is eliminating the commute. Employees save hours a day sitting in a car, bus, or train just trying to get to work. Commuting takes energy and more importantly time. From a pragmatic point of view, it is much easier to ask an employee to work a couple of hours of overtime if they have more hours to give.

Eliminating commute times conserves individual energy and helps alleviate fatigue. It can also help relieve stress. Daily commutes can be a large source of frustration and can cause stress which is draining. Remote work, even part of the time can help employees be more relaxed, refreshed, and in the long run, more productive. People who are stress free experience greater job satisfaction and are less likely to look for a new job, which can help reduce employee churn.

The saved time can also help employees reconnect with loved ones and even exercise more. Although healthy and happy employees are not normally a key business differentiator it is intuitive to innovative companies that improving the lives of the individual contributors in the business will improve their performance at work.

By removing geography from the equation "office workers" are also able to schedule their work around their personal schedules. Some people work better in the evenings or early mornings. They can work when they are most productive and not worry about punching a clock at a preset time; they may get in their work time between one and three a.m. If they need to work overtime, it is much easier to do so from their home office.

Remote work will also help alleviate most of the effects of weather-based shut downs by allowing workers to work from wherever they are rather than try to brave a snow storm so that they don't lose a personal day. Companies will experience an uptick in "virtual" attendance and lower rates of absenteeism. Employees will be available.

Demographic changes are also impacting businesses. The 2010 census showed that the United States grew by 23.7 million a 9.7 percent increase from 2000-2010. Buried in the data were some startling trends that are important for business owners. Large population centers like New York, Los Angeles, and Houston continued to grow by double digits, while new construction actually declined. The housing decline from 2008-2012 was no secret, but what may not be quite as obvious is commercial construction starts were also in decline.

An ever increasing population with lower new construction will eventually mean an increase in the cost of commercial real estate and increase in local housing costs. It is simple supply and demand and comes with intrinsic costs to businesses. The cost of hiring employees locally goes up as well as the cost of commercial real estate.

Implementing a remote work program can help companies reduce their real estate costs. They can reduce the amount of office space they purchase in urban areas and move some of their workers to home offices or even to lower cost rural areas with no loss in productivity. Some companies are even choosing to eliminate their office space altogether and go completely virtual.

Companies with multiple locations that use technology to integrate their communications can achieve economies of scale otherwise impossible. For example a law firm with four locations may employ as many as eight executive assistants for call coverage. Four of the assistants are full time and the other four of them have part-time responsibility during, breaks, lunch, and vacations. By integrating all four offices as remote locations, all inbound calls for the entire firm can be handled from a single location if desired, with back up assistance from any of the other locations at any time. E-mail, phone coverage, file data, and calendars can be shared across all four locations.

Remote work can help companies hire the best people no matter where they are located. It alleviates the need for relocation and increases the pool of qualified workers from just the local area to nationwide. Companies with a footprint in large urban areas will also find their hiring costs reduced as many recruiters in rural areas are lower cost.

Another advantage of remote work is wage arbitration. Knowledge workers in lower cost regions can be engaged to do work in more expensive urban areas. For instance a Manhattan-based firm can hire a remote receptionist from Helena, Montana to handle all inbound calls. Wage differences between Montana and New York could automatically create a win for both parties. This trend is even extending overseas in some enterprises but there are many challenges both technologically and linguistically.

A major difference between Generation X and Y is how they think about the separation of their work and personal lives. Those in Generation X have embraced the idea of blurring their work and home life, but Generation Y has taken it to a new level. The idea of being in the office and working against a clock is less and less tolerable to a younger more technology savvy group, and the idea of working for work's sake is less and less the mainstay of the work day. Generation Y is much more likely to work hours outside the normal eight to six model and work when it is most convenient and productive to them and their lives.

Another advantage of remote work assignments is the elimination of time wasting activities that are a common part of office life: coworkers talking about the big game last night, needless meetings, interruptions, jokes, coffee breaks, etc. Efficiency studies have pointed out that it is not unusual for an individual to spend twenty minutes a day just preparing to work and another sixty to ninety minutes a day socializing with coworkers. Remote work minimizes this type of waste factor on a daily basis. If remote work just reduced the amount of socializing time by thirty minutes a day, over the course of an entire year it could increase individual productivity by more than an entire work week.

Obstacles to Remote Work

Remote work is not for everyone. Individuals need an environment where they can focus without interruption. Young children and other distractions can make it impossible to make working from home a viable option. It also takes a certain amount of self-discipline and a self-starter type attitude. Some individuals are easily distracted and taking a mid-morning nap or watching television will be an insurmountable lure when they need to be working and can easily sabotage their productivity.

Many leaders new to remote work are reluctant to let employees out of their physical sight out of fear of goofing off. But, activity monitoring is relatively easy to implement using the right technology tools. Presence monitoring software, e-mail, call logs, and video make it easy for managers to do periodic check-ins on their staff and keep close tabs on activity levels.

It is also helpful to establish daily and weekly objectives that employees and managers agree upon in advance. Management by objective removes the urge to link time spent at a given moment to value gained by a knowledge worker when they are at their best.

Before moving an individual to a full-time remote work assignment it is best to test it on a part-time basis. Pick a day of the week, like Friday, to start and monitor the progress closely. How is their performance on Friday? Is it better than normal or at least the same? How did they feel about working alone? For some people the isolation of remote work is a drawback from going to the office.

Remote Work Requirements

In order for an employee to work remotely, a few tools need to be in place. As I mentioned before, they need a good working environment and it needs to be capable of supporting the technology they need to be successful.

The first technology requirement of remote work outside of a computer is a good broadband connection. The Internet speed of the home office will often dictate success. This is not nearly as big of an obstacle today as it was five years ago, but in some rural areas, high speed Internet is still not widely available. The employee will need to do an assessment of their Internet versus what remote tools they will be using. If they need to run voice, video, and data a high speed pipe is vital. But if they are going to use their cell phone for voice and just connect to a file server sometimes then a slower Internet connection might serve them well.

Also, the Internet connection needs to include the option of a hard cable. Wireless Internet does not always work well with telephony and video. Both are bandwidth heavy and directly connecting to a router will improve the user experience.

The second major tool of the remote worker is connection to the data and software they need to be productive. The question to ask is where is data located and how will they access it? Many companies use file servers located either in their office or in a data center and the remote employee will need a software program that allows them to connect securely. Some companies are foregoing file servers and incorporating hosted SaaS programs that can be accessed through any Internet connection without the need for special software.

The third tool is software. Many companies have software that they run on their own servers. Remote workers need access to proprietary software. Access can be achieved in much the same way as access to a file server, but software running across the Internet can be frustrating due to lag times if not properly set up. Some software programs are just not good candidates for remote work. It is always best to test an idea's viability.

The bottom line is remote work is no longer something incredibly new. It is quickly becoming a common business practice. Remote work is a game changer for individuals and companies from a productivity point of view and it also can contribute to *Cracking Disaster Recovery*.

CLUES TO CRACKING THE CODE

▶ Good bandwidth is the first requirement in determining if someone can work remotely.

▶ What technology tools are required to help the remote worker be productive?

▶ What are the success criteria of remote workers?

▶ Test new remote workers with a part-time schedule before committing to a full-time remote schedule.

CHAPTER NINE

•————————————•

Cracking Disaster Recovery

During disasters, the main super villain of IT attacks is Outage. He is the business destroyer. In February of 2010, two back-to-back blizzards slammed the entire northeastern United States. The storms dropped more than four feet of snow in some areas and caused the shutdown of all government agencies in the capital. In New York, the Long Island Rail Road reported that commuter traffic was down by more than 46 percent. As many as a million people were prevented from going to work due to the weather. Businesses, government agencies, schools, and universities were all shuttered. Several estimates calculated that in the government sector alone more than $100 billion in productivity was lost. There is not a clear calculation of lost productivity in the private sector, but it conceivably topped the $250 billion mark.

Major events such as the terrorist attacks of September 11, 2001; the 2003 blackout in the northeastern United States; Hurricane Katrina; and the California wildfires are other case studies in the need for developing comprehensive disaster recovery plans.

These are unusual events. They make headlines because they are dramatic and all-encompassing and they are also the exception. Disasters of such widespread and long duration are few and far between. But, in all these events, many businesses were stopped in their tracks with no recourse to continue doing business for weeks at a time. Some ended up closing their doors because they could not recover. They needed disaster recovery plans before an event occurred. Many companies lost access to their facilities completely for days or even weeks at a time, and for a few unlucky companies their location was badly damaged or even destroyed.

Every business needs at least basic disaster recovery protection, but many small businesses do not have the resources to develop a major disaster recovery plan that can take into account all scenarios. When resources are limited, a more pragmatic approach is necessary.

The number one goal of a disaster recovery plan is to preserve the profitability of the business when something goes wrong. The actions taken will generally depend on the type of disruption and the duration. A few basic precautions can go a long way toward maintaining the viability of the business.

Think of DR as active insurance. You are taking pragmatic action—not just a financial hedge toward alleviating the damage an event can cause you and your business. With that in mind, there are three areas businesses need to focus on in their disaster recovery planning: voice, data, and computing. Voice is generally the first line of communication with customers. It encompasses the company's phone numbers and phone system. Data is the company's vital information: digital documents, customer information, financial information, etc. It is the life blood of the company and by far the most difficult to replace if lost. Last, but not least, is the company's computing power. It is comprised of the laptop and desktop computers of the company, as well as the network equipment that enables them to run and connect to the Internet and one another.

More than one type of DR plan is necessary. Each plan is scenario and time based and addresses the company's reaction to a specific disruption in one of the three areas. It will also encompass individual and company-wide needs. The depth of planning and the resources required are dictated by the needs of the company and the cost of an outage. For example, a financial company engaged in high frequency trading may invest in fully redundant systems to prevent even one minute of disruption. In some cases they may even purchase alternate office space that is ready to be occupied on a moment's notice. While in contrast, a professional services company whose primary function is person to person may make very little investment and take relatively simple steps to alleviate an outage.

A DR planning matrix is an easy way to get started. The most common disruptions that need planning are file server issues and Internet outages.

Event Type	Users Affected	Action
Internet Outage	multiple	If duration > 3 hours send everyone home to work remotely
Major virus/Hack	multiple	call IT support; prepare back ups; send personnel home
Local Power Outage	multiple	if < 1 hour work off of local back up power
Regional Power Outage	multiple	if > 1 hour send everyone home to work remotely as practical
Phone System Failure	multiple	Call carrier and RCF main line to cell phones
Server Failure	multiple	Use back ups to rebuild server locally or in cloud computer crashes single restore from back up
Computer Crashes	single	Restore from back up

DATA PLANNING: Where data is located and how it is accessed matters. For instance, companies that move 100 percent to a cloud model accept loss of access risk during Internet outages. Internet availability becomes a single point of failure. Some companies will invest in purchasing a redundant connection from a different provider to alleviate the risk of Internet loss. Others choose a hybrid cloud-premise model where a cloud server is linked to a local file server. If the local server has issues the backup server can be accessed through the connections. Many times cloud servers can provide a poor user experience due to latency and bandwidth issues.

A redundant server is different than data back up! Data backup is normally accomplished with versioning over time to provide the ability to restore a file from a previous point in time weeks or even months before the current version. Tape backup is dying a slow death and being replaced by low cost local and cloud storage.

COMPUTING PLANNING: The ugly truth is that over a long enough timeline, all equipment fails. And even worse, predicting the time of failure is nearly impossible. Anything can happen—drops, spills, theft, or just bad luck and the drive fails. Whatever the cause, you must plan for your next replacement computer now. As a rule of thumb, computers will need to be replaced every three to four years.

TELEPHONY PLANNING: Widespread use of cell phones has made planning for telephone issues much easier. The simplest plans just direct customers and staff to alternate phone numbers. Depending on the business, in the case of call centers, user groups, etc., very intricate telephony planning is possible with remote call forwards to redundant locations and back up lines if required.

How to prepare?

- Keep a record of your software licenses and types of software on the computer.

- Keep a record of where your software copies are stored (physically or digitally).

- Record the serial number of your computer and warranty information.

- Ensure data is backed up on the company server or directly using a backup client.

- Keep records of all passwords: computers, firewalls, servers, switches, domain controller, etc.

It is helpful to keep at least one physical copy of all information. If you have a general event and all the records were digital you could be in trouble.

Disaster recovery planning is mostly common sense. The most important thing is to think through scenarios by duration. By planning for the worst in advance, the chances of staying in business after a disaster are greatly improved. The next step is to evaluate what company to assist you in your expertise gaps. It begins with choosing the right partner and understanding *Outsourcing Secrets*.

CLUES TO CRACKING THE CODE

▶ Start with the company backups. Data is the most difficult asset to replace or recover.

▶ Do not be intimidated by technical jargon. Keep it simple. Continuously ask yourself the question, if X happens, how does it affect our business?

▶ Planning for hardware refreshes on a schedule will greatly reduce the need, and therefore cost, of initiating a major disaster recovery operation.

CHAPTER TEN

•————————•

The Dilemma: Hire or Outsource?

D o you have a Vice President of Electricity in your company today? No? Well in the very near future, CIOs and CTOs may very well be lumped in the same category at the local business museum. In much the same way as electricity became something that every company bought from a third party, IT is quickly following the same path. As we covered in chapters 2-4, a single in-house IT professional can be expensive and introduce unnecessary risk into the company. It raises the question, what are the options and how do we execute those options?

Before discussing how to outsource, it may be helpful to address an outsourcing obstacle that starts in the minds of business leaders. Some business owners have real difficulty giving up their intimate control of a vital company function. There is a comfortable feeling of having someone physically present to help with issues on the spot. It is not a wrong feeling, but it comes with real cost. Hiring a full-time resource who is only partially used is incredibly expensive and it often leads to disappointment.

Working with an outsourced provider is a slightly different experience. Many of the issues will be handled remotely through a remote connection and a phone call. If done right resolution times can be greatly reduced because an in hour resource can only handle a single issue at a time while an outside provider may be able to handle many issues simultaneously.

Because of the way most companies rate their IT department, speed to resolution often becomes *the* key performance indicator, when in fact, prevention is much more cost effective over the long term. An outsourced provider should have significantly more help desk resources than a single IT provider and will be able to react to issues much faster. Most outsourced companies use software programs that allow them to log into a computer or server remotely, which increases their efficiency. By removing the need to travel to the actual customer's location, a single professional can efficiently handle many more issues than one who is traveling and meeting with clients face to face.

What changes is the way the communication around the issue occurs. Typically the process will begin with an e-mail or phone call that opens a ticket and lets the provider know what information is available about the issue. They then take the information and begin the troubleshooting process. It is an extremely cost effective and efficient model.

Remote Support Flow

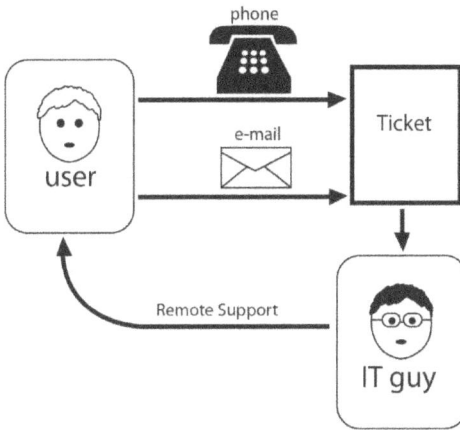

Once you get used to the system and work with a provider who has good follow up and service, you will be surprised at how well it works. But it all starts with the ability to let go of the function. It is a very similar dilemma that companies faced when outsourced payroll first started. Traditionally, companies processed their own payroll in-house, but the logistics of running payroll is expensive and cumbersome if it is not your core business. After struggling with many of the same philosophical issues of outsourcing IT, many companies outsource their payroll.

If, while calculating your costs in chapter 3, you came to the determination that fully outsourcing your IT is not cost effective and you are sure the risks associated with in-house IT are acceptable, you will still want to consider outsourcing certain project work.

There are two projects companies should avoid undertaking on their own: e-mail and server migrations. In both cases the cost associated with problems and issues are far too high. The projects are often very difficult and most importantly, it will most likely be the one and only time your team will do the project. It doesn't make practical sense to subject your company to the risk associated of being the test case of your IT department. For most managed service providers, they will have tested and rehearsed how to do a similar migration that you are attempting many times before they work on your project. If the new technology is more than three to four months old, they may have already successfully completed dozens of migrations before starting work on yours. That type of experience is extremely valuable. They will be much faster to resolution than your team and very often they will know about issues that are not published in the deployment instructions from the vendor.

Who do you want to perform your open heart surgery? The surgeon who is just starting out or the surgeon who has a wall full of thank you notes from previous successes?

Expertise is one of the main reasons outsourced providers are such a good value. Very often their time to resolution will be a fraction of what an in-house team can accomplish. Companies who hire staff to cover multiple disciplines are inefficient. There is a lot of figuring out what needs to be done as things come up. Jobs can take two, or even three, times longer than an expert would to accomplish the same task.

Managed service providers are able to hire specialists and spread their expertise among a group of customers. It is a more efficient way of allocating the resource and lowers the risk of projects. The difference between a true expert working on a project versus a generalist with a working knowledge can be the difference between the success or failure of a project.

A company with access to an expert who is at the top of their field just when they need him is key to lowering risk and ultimately to lowering costs. The risk is lower because, more likely than not, the expert has seen just about everything that can go wrong and knows what needs to be done to avoid or correct the issue. The initial cost of hiring an expert is generally higher than a generalist and cost savings are achieved through the efficiency of how fast they are able to work and the problems they avoid.

Choosing a Partner

Technology support companies or as they call themselves, Managed Services Providers (MSPs), come in three different buckets. As an industry, they are similar to the accounting industry in that there is a pyramid of providers. There are a few very large companies at the top of the pyramid, a few hundred mid-sized firms, and then, at the bottom, thousands of small mom and pop type operations with less than ten employees. All three can be a good value depending on the size and complexity of the service that is needed. The main criterion is to choose an IT partner that fits your budget and needs for the next one to three years. Bringing on a new IT provider is a project that requires focus and energy and no matter who you choose there will be a honeymoon period where you both get used to each other and establish a working relationship.

MSP Types

LARGE: Very large MSPs come with deep resources. They are the one stop shop for specialty IT. They are usually more expensive than mid-sized firms and small firms, but not always. Their biggest strength is service variety and the ability to provide nationally and even globally. They can cover many different types of complex service issues on an around the clock basis without needing to engage a third party provider. And they manage each different sub-specialty themselves. They are a very compelling value for large companies with many different needs across a large geography.

Downside: Sometimes the nature of the service does not mesh well with small businesses. It tends to be less personal and getting odd issues solved can be a frustrating process.

MID-SIZED: The middle tier of the IT pyramid tends to be regional. They will cover a specific geography such as a city, county, or in some areas, a driving radius of their headquarters. They come with a solid mix of services that will cover the needs of some enterprises and nearly all SMBs. Sometimes they will offer around the clock service and they will tend to have more partner relationships to cover technology areas that they do not carry in-house.

Downside: Mid-sized firms run into growing pains. When they have employee churn it can cascade down to their customers in a broad way. They can also be risky when they are attempting to add a new capability and roll it out to customers too early. They tend to be solid businesses with longevity in the market place.

SMALL: Small firms come in two different sub-categories: lifestyle businesses and growing practices. Lifestyle businesses are usually one to three engineers who provide basic IT support locally and growing practices continue to add capabilities and technical support. Both are very often much lower cost than mid-sized and large firms and can be a good value if your needs are fairly straight forward, 8:00 a.m. to 6:00 p.m., Monday to Friday.

Downside: Lifestyle businesses come and go. Entrepreneurial life is difficult at best and many of these businesses were started by engineers who were dissatisfied with their current job, grabbed a few customers, and struck out on their own. They very often underprice their services to get started and never make enough money to grow or pay themselves well. Growing practices are a little more stable, but they are more likely to provide poor service. They are so resource constrained that when they have employee churn there is no back fill. If everyone else is fully utilized and your account manager left the firm, who is left to help you?

There are many different types of technology providers, and a careful review of their capabilities and how they align with the needs of your business will help you select the best one for your needs. Next to help round out your understanding of the technology code is *The Mystery of Telephony.*

CLUES TO CRACKING THE CODE

•————————————————•

▶ Build your outside partnerships before you need them.

▶ Ask how many employees they have and how long they have been in business.

▶ Request professional CTO/CIO help for planning and budgeting purpose.

▶ Compare prices but focus on overall value.

•————————————————•

CHAPTER ELEVEN

•————————•

The Mystery of Telephony

The computing and telephony worlds are converging. Phone systems were once a nearly pure hardware solution and now they are transforming to a nearly pure software solution. The Internet has made it possible to forgo purchasing a premise based phone system (PBX) and, much like a SaaS program, subscribe to a phone service. Currently the puzzle for most companies is whether or not to buy a phone system or to use a cloud provider. In the beginning, hosted providers played to the weakness of the PBX industry. The PBX was difficult to administer (many still are) and the features and functionalities took a telephony expert to keep them running correctly. They were expensive to purchase and very expensive to run and that was before companies even paid for the usage to their carrier.

Hosted providers offered a much simpler system. Users could subscribe to the service, in most cases purchasing only handsets and through an easy to use internet portal they could administer the system themselves. The systems were so easy to use and administer they could actually get more functionality out of the system than many PBXs just because they understood more about what it could do and how they could use it. And the price was very attractive. Most providers moved to a flat rate, unlimited calling plan that included the cost of support and minutes and so the total cost of ownership of a hosted system over a five year horizon in many cases was much cheaper than a PBX.

By and large, the premise based phone system (PBX) manufacturers are in trouble. Nortel, once Canada's largest PBX manufacturer, filed for bankruptcy in 2009 and was quickly bought out by Avaya. It was the shot across the bow for the entire industry that the cloud is a real threat to the PBX business model. Hosted VoIP companies are increasingly taking market share from their premise based rivals and grew revenues by an astounding 193.9 percent from 2000 to 2011, while their premise based rivals generally saw declines in market share.

The response of PBX manufacturers, most notably Avaya and Shoretel was to simplify their systems, introduce portal based management and to lower the costs of their hardware. They innovated to make the five year cost of ownership of a premise based system more on par with a hosted VoIP system, and they were helped by downward pressure on the price of minutes. Innovation and the lower cost of calls has leveled the playing field between hosted VoIP and PBX ownership.

So how do you decide between a Hosted System and a PBX?

The first clue to help you solve the telephony puzzle for your business is to review your current phone bill. How many minutes does your company use a month and how much do you pay per minute? These numbers are the first key to unlocking the puzzle. Remember, we are starting from the assumption that the functionality of the PBX or hosted VoIP system you choose are virtually the same.

Next we are going to calculate the five year cost of hardware and service and compare them. You will need to approach two or three vendors in each category and ask them for a quote. In general, for each system you will need the costs for the following:

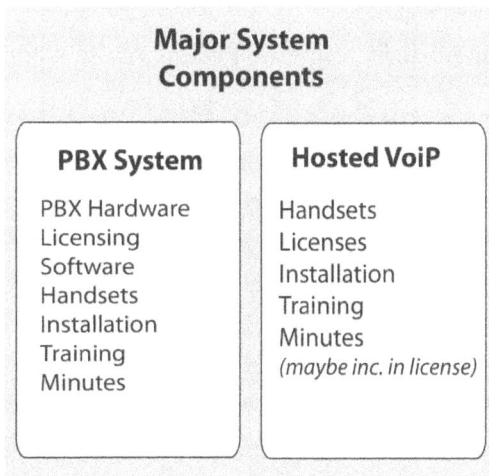

Major System Components

PBX System	Hosted VoIP
PBX Hardware	Handsets
Licensing	Licenses
Software	Installation
Handsets	Training
Installation	Minutes
Training	*(maybe inc. in license)*
Minutes	

Keep in mind that for the PBX the price of minutes will not normally come from the PBX reseller. It will come from your local telephone company. For Hosted VoIP you will need to carefully review the offering of each vendor separately as some of them bundle their minutes into the seat price and others may charge separately for minutes or a combination of the two.

Once you have the comparable costs there are a few other factors to consider. The first is capacity planning and waste factor. Waste factor is a drawback of a PBX and must be thought through carefully. You must understand your five year business plan and have a rough estimate of the number of people who will be using the system.

The PBX must be oversized to allow for growth and when the maximum size is exceeded, it will require additional expenditure to increase capacity. For example, if a system is sized with a 10 percent overage, the excess capacity goes unused until growth occurs to utilize the excess capacity. If the business contracts for one reason or another, the waste factor of the PBX increases with it.

If growth exceeds the business plan, it may trigger the need for an additional upgrade, or replacement of the entire system. Companies that are growing quickly face a major capacity planning headache to ensure the waste factor is minimized. Another scenario that can effect capacity planning is during an acquisition. Often two companies may have incompatible systems and unifying the communications of the two companies can become a puzzle in and of itself. One system may not have enough capacity for both companies or if there was a downsizing the result might be a large amount of excess capacity that is pure waste factor.

Hosted VoIP eliminates much of the waste factor. With most providers you pay as you go, for only the services you need at a given moment. If you add ten new users you pay for ten users. If ten users are downsized, within minutes the system can be downsized with them. Companies faced with reducing costs are able to do so much more efficiently than a company that has already sunk a fortune into hardware. Each hosted VoIP vendor will have its own policy regarding removing profiles during the contract, but many of them allow it within a certain range.

The next consideration is the number of locations. When getting your quotes from each vendor you will need to understand how the systems will integrate with each other and what the additional soft costs of managing the system across locations are. Depending on the number and size of locations you may need to buy multiple PBXs. With more than three locations it is not unusual for the price of the PBX system to be far more than the Hosted VoIP proposal.

The number of home users or locations with fewer than five users also needs to be considered. Users can generally work remotely with a handset that is configured to work through the Internet. You will need to review the type and amount of bandwidth at each location to ensure it is adequate. For the PBX solution, that user will need to have access to a central office remotely. The call will go through their Internet to the main office and then out to the telephone network. If the Internet is down, or the main office is having trouble, then the remote user will also have trouble. Hosted VoIP customers can generally work from any Internet connection and with adequate bandwidth the experience will be the same as in the office. One small drawback of remote users on a PBX is that it increases the complexity of the system. Remote users will usually connect using a VPN connection which will need to be configured and maintained by an IT professional. If the remote user is having difficulty, troubleshooting can be complicated.

One other drawback of the PBX to keep in mind is the same as the ownership of any equipment. It is subject to the perils of fire, flood, theft, catastrophic failure, user error, damage, and the myriad of problems associated with ownership. It must be safeguarded, managed, and insured, all of which are outside of the core functions and profit centers of the business. In essence, hardware ownership can be a drain on resources and, if difficult to manage, a distraction to the staff.

Choosing a Hosted VoIP Provider

Most hosted VoIP providers appear nearly identical on paper—there are just so many ways to design a robust technology platform. Most of the difference is in the structure of their business. With a few notable exceptions, hosted VoIP providers are running software platforms they lease from other companies. They didn't design the software they are using and their understanding of how that software works and what problems they may encounter varies widely. Their ability to troubleshoot complex technical issues can be limited. They rarely have the ability to customize an application for an enterprise with a special need or to integrate a major new application such as a custom CRM package or database of some sort.

Experience is another vital issue in the Hosted VoIP arena. Many hosted VoIP companies are spin offs from technology companies that traditionally specialized in local area networks, desktop support, IT consulting, or even Broadband providers. They jumped on the VoIP bandwagon as a growing trend in the marketplace. They saw it as an opportunity to expand their business because of its delivery through the LAN, but it is a very different business and often the hosted VoIP side of their business will suffer.

Hosted VoIP on first look seems to be an extension of traditional IT work. But this cannot be further from the truth. Tying the Public Switch Telephone Network (PSTN) to private networks and delivering advanced call control to businesses is an extremely specialized field of knowledge. Vendor management is quite different in the telecom industry than in most other technical fields and can be a difficult transition for companies trying to bridge the learning gap. The telecom world has its own idiosyncratic language and processes that are baffling to outsiders and makes it more difficult for new comers to navigate.

To help evaluate different providers, this simple evaluation model divides them into three separate tiers. The tiers, in and of themselves, do not necessarily make one better than another, but they act as a differentiation point. The three tiers are a useful lens for you to evaluate a potential provider and understand if their current business capabilities are the right fit for you and your business now.

TIER 1: Providers who own their own proprietary platform and run service across private networks. They tend to have deep expertise in software design and in telecom management. These providers tend to be at the higher end of the cost scale, but are able to deliver a premium in reliability, integration, customization, and service. In general, they are the safest choice for reliability.

TIER 2: Providers who lease their platform from a software developer and run service across private networks. Their expertise is normally less than Tier 1 providers but they can provide reliable service. They tend to be slightly lower cost than Tier 1 providers, but do not normally have the flexibility to customize solutions for enterprise clients and have limited advanced services, integration capability, and customization. They can be a reliable choice.

TIER 3: Providers who generally provide service through the open Internet. If they do offer service through a private network it is limited. Their expertise is typically very low and rarely offer advanced services, integration and customization. Their strength is in their low cost. They can be effective for companies with fewer than ten employees who are looking for some advanced capabilities. These companies can minimize the downside impact of network outages and disruptions. In general, they are not a *good fit* for companies with more than eight to ten users at a single location.

Choosing the right provider for your needs is easy if you know the right questions to ask. Consider the following evaluation questions.

How long has the company been in business?

This is an important question to help understand if the provider has a successful track record or is a startup. Being a startup is not necessarily a disqualifier, but it is a risk factor to consider. If they suddenly go out of business, are the handsets they support easily transferable to another provider? One common mistake companies make is that they choose a provider who only supports a niche proprietary handset, and not an industry standard. The handsets become an additional barrier from moving from one provider to another.

What is their business plan?

How they see themselves growing as a business will either add or remove risk from the choice. If their singular focus is on voice and expanding in a deliberate manner, then the risk is slightly lower than if they offer several products, one of which happens to be Hosted VoIP, and they have an aggressive plan to expand nationally or internationally. Overexpansion is perhaps one of the most common business mistakes. Focus is important. Hosted VoIP is an easy concept on a white board and very difficult to implement well in the real world.

How many clients similar to your business are they currently supporting?

This is an important question to help you get a feel for if they understand your industry's specific needs. For instance, I have visited dozens of law firms and nearly all of them have the same basic business process. They bill much of their time on the phone. They use some sort of system to track partner time for billing purposes and generally will have administrative assistants assigned to a single partner or a group of partners. Their phone system and ease of use is core to their business. If for instance, you are running a law firm and the provider supports several similarly sized law firms, chances are they will have some experience handling advanced call coverage across multiple executive assistants and will be familiar with how many partners like to work. If you are running a one hundred seat hedge fund with over twenty ring downs and your provider doesn't currently support any financial companies, then they probably are unfamiliar with your disaster recovery needs.

Ask for references that are not listed on their website. The website references will all be positive—that is why they are there. You want to test how deep their positive references go. Reference checks that are three and four deep become difficult for companies with a short track record. You can save yourself a lot of pain and suffering by digging deeper than just the surface.

If they do not have the track record then you have a decision point. Is their price point and overall track record worth the risk to you to be an early adopter of their service? At this point, you might look at other clients they have who are in a somewhat similar industry such as professional services of some sort.

What resources are available to address a technology issue?

Regardless of which vendor is being used, problems will inevitably crop up. The provider must have the engineering and system design resources to quickly and efficiently address the issue. The most common difficulties companies experience are problems with connectivity at the local level, such as when the broadband connection goes down, integration issues, and compatibility issues.

For hosted VoIP companies a few questions can help discern among the providers up front:

1. What network monitoring are they doing of your connection?

2. What carrier relationships do they have in place to open and oversee work orders to correct deficiencies?

3. Do they have a written escalation process?

4. How many data centers are they running and are they completely redundant?

How many employees do they have?

If it is a company with only a few employees, say ten and under, then they may have difficulty reacting quickly to issues in a timely manner. If they do not have strong pull with their vendors, who in the hosted VoIP case might be Verizon or AT&T, then getting issues solved quickly could be a challenge and it might be wise to consider a larger provider.

How do they accomplish application integration?

Applications (APPs for short) are the future of the entire telecommunications and computing industries. They are the secret sauce that make for wonderful and unexpected capabilities. Deep integration with all types of other technologies can take a somewhat simple device like an iPad and change it into a productive tool with vast business capabilities. If they do not have a platform for integrating with CRM systems, and other types of databases, and that is something you need now or in the future, then move on to another provider. A company that is selling cookie cutter service with no APP capability is probably not set up to support the business in other areas. The lack of depth in integration with other applications is not always a roadblock. It is a consideration. As I mentioned before, some companies just resell another provider's platform or are a pass through agent renting licenses from a prime vendor and can be quite cost effective. The important part is to realize the limitation and decide if it is acceptable for your business at this time. Vanilla may have been your mother's favorite flavor because it was safe and what she always loved, but if your business needs a rocky road banana split then you need to look elsewhere.

What is their technology roadmap?

Having a technology roadmap will say a lot about a potential company. First, it will say they have a thoughtful management team with a vision of the future that a company may be able to benefit from down the road. It will give you the opportunity to grow with a good vendor. The roadmap also says the company's financials are probably fairly solid. Companies rarely invest in R&D if they are short on cash or do not have a good pipeline of business coming in the door and have a reason for developing something new. There are certainly exceptions—RIM comes to mind. The road map also points to a deep knowledge and understanding of the business that is just lacking in companies without a roadmap. In most of the resellers they just won't have a clue, making it easy to quickly ascertain if they are a Tier 1 or Tier 2 provider. A Tier 2 provider may be fine, and in some cases they may be lower cost, but they come with added risk and it may require a change in providers down the road.

Choosing between a PBX or a Hosted VoIP provider is easy if you follow the clues. Don't allow marketing puffery to get in the way of the real issues. Both the PBX manufacturers and Hosted VoIP providers make bold and provocative proclamations about the other, such as "The PBX is dead!" Or "Hosted VoIP is new, risky, and doesn't work." But both of them have their own use cases, strengths, and weaknesses.

CLUES TO CRACKING THE CODE

▶ Start the process with the current total costs of telephone.

▶ Calculate the total cost of ownership over three to five years when comparing a premise based system with a Hosted VoIP system.

▶ Choose the provider who is a good fit and the right risk profile for your business, not just the lowest cost.

CONCLUSION

•————————•

No single book could possibly cover all technology management possibilities or issues. My hope was to give you a framework to cover the basics. I originally started to create a detailed guide in how to select Marketing Automation systems and CRM systems and realized many companies do not have a need and the technical details would be lost on most people. But if you by chance find you may have a need for that, please reach out and I can help.

Check out www.candoideas.com/itcode for some free tools to help you get started in *Cracking the IT Code* and please do not hesitate to contact me with your questions and comments for future updates of the book at Anthony@candoideas.com.

ABOUT THE AUTHOR

•————————•

Anthony L. Butler is a lifelong technologist who took apart his first computer and wrote his first code when he was fourteen. He has founded three businesses and is the former CEO of one of the 100 largest IT companies in the country. He is a professional speaker and as a combat veteran and graduate of the United States Military Academy at West Point, his talk, "Combat Leadership for Business" has garnered rave reviews as well as his talks on "Technology Management and Success." Often described as the CTO or Chief Translation Officer, his greatest skill may be the ability to take a complex technological idea and make it easy to understand. He is the author of numerous articles on leadership, sales, marketing, and technology. On a personal note, he is also a champion Brazilian Jiu-Jitsu competitor and an Ultimate Fighting Championship fanatic. He is married with two young sons and lives in Connecticut. To book him as a speaker or to inquire about bulk book discounts, please contact him at anthony@candoideas.com.

9 781941 870129